Writing and Sense of Self

D1430462

College Section Committee

Tilly Warnock, Chair, University of Wyoming
Lil Brannon, SUNY at Albany
Doris O. Ginn, Jackson State University
Brenda M. Greene, Medgar Evers College, CUNY
Linda H. Peterson, Yale University
James F. Slevin, Georgetown University
Joseph F. Trimmer, Ball State University
Art Young, Clemson University
James Raymond, ex officio, University of Alabama
H. Thomas McCracken, CEE Representative, Youngstown State
    University
Janet Emig, Executive Committee Liaison, Rutgers University

Writing and Sense of Self

Identity Negotiation in Writing Workshops

Robert E. Brooke
University of Nebraska–Lincoln

National Council of Teachers of English
1111 Kenyon Road, Urbana, Illinois 61801

Cover Design: Doug Burnett

Interior Design: Tom Kovacs for TGK Design

Staff Editor: Sheila A. Ryan

NCTE Stock Number: 58692-3020

Library of Congress Cataloging-in-Publication Data
Brooke, Robert Edward.
  Writing and sense of self : identity negotiation in writing
workshops / Robert E. Brooke.
      p.   cm.
  Includes bibliographical references and index.
  ISBN 0-8141-5869-2
  1. English language—Rhetoric—Study and teaching—Psychological
aspects. 2. English language—Composition and exercises—Study and
teaching (Secondary)—Psychological aspects. 3. Identity
(Psychology) I. National Council of Teachers of English.
II. Title.
PE1404.B755   1991
808'.042'019—dc20   90-24286
                                                              CIP

Contents

Acknowledgments

Writing only becomes meaningful in social interaction, in discussion, thinking, and collaboration with others we respect. Writers do not write by and for themselves; they write to respond to others, to figure out what they think, to contribute to tasks they share with colleagues. This book, *Writing and Sense of Self,* emerged from a particularly rich cooperative environment—one which I would like to acknowledge here.

When I came to the University of Nebraska as a new Ph.D., I was already thinking about identity issues as they applied to writing. I had spent a good deal of my graduate program reading identity theory and pondering how writing connected with identity development. But I lacked a context for this thinking, a shared and cooperative network of other teachers and writers who also pondered these matters. For me, such a context was offered by the University of Nebraska. Here, I found myself part of an exciting and energetic group of teachers who were probing some of the same questions I was—and probing them first and foremost through their classroom practice, their daily inter- actions with students.

My colleagues at Nebraska provided the context for this book in a number of ways. Some colleagues, including Les Whipp, Bob Bergstrom, and Barbara DiBernard, modeled ways of teaching which showed that academic work could connect directly with students' lives. Others, including Gerry Brookes, Kate Ronald, Judy Levin, Anne Whitney, and the members of the Composition Colloquium, formed a community of teacher-reader-writers with the hope that education could be im- proved, locally and nationally. Still others, including Ruth Mirtz, Tom O'Connor, and Bob Haller, worked with me on collaborative projects in the hope of understanding our students and our teaching better. This lively community made it important and exciting to continue writing, teaching, and thinking, because what one did in these areas really mattered to others.

But most important for the development of this book was my friendship and collaboration with Joy Ritchie. In 1986, Joy and I began an informal research project by participating in each other's classes and talking with each other once a week about those classes. Since that time, we have worked closely together, collaborating on research, team-teaching in the Nebraska Writing Project, serving on seemingly endless university committees. We have continued our informal discussions about our teaching and our goals, and it is directly from these discussions that the formative ideas of this book emerged. Without my continued conversation and collaboration with her, this book would never have developed. I wrote with her imagined response in mind, and I suspect the book would only have been better if we had more directly coauthored it.

I would also like to acknowledge other kinds of support for the writing of this book. A very incomplete first draft was supported by a Cora Friedline Faculty Summer Fellowship. Portions of the book have appeared in significantly different forms in several publications. A more extended analysis of the class described in chapter 3 appeared in *Audience Expectations and Teacher Demands* (Robert Brooke and John Hendricks, Carbondale, Ill.: Conference on College Composition and Communication/Southern Illinois University Press, 1989). Different approaches to the class described in chapter 4 appeared in "Underlife and Writing Instruction" (*College Composition and Communication* 38 [1987]:141–153) and in "Modeling a Writer's Identity" (*CCC* 39 [1988]:23–41). An extended analysis of the class presented in chapter 6 appeared in Joy Ritchie's "Beginning Writers: Diverse Voices and Individual Identity" (*CCC* 40 [1989]:152–174).

1 Learning and Identity Negotiation: A Key to Understanding Writing Instruction

This book came about because of a shift in my teaching, a shift I have been since trying to understand.

In 1986 I changed the structure of my writing classes from a sequential curriculum to a writing workshop. Where I had designed my classes as a sequence of assignments demonstrating rhetorical principles, I substituted a workshop in which the students and I choose our own topics and tempos for writing, developing our work within a predictable structure of group response and idea exploration.

This shift in classroom structure required a similar shift in my sense of mission as a teacher. I had conceived of myself as someone who understood rhetorical principles and could teach them by designing writing activities in which students discover the usefulness of those principles. I took on a new conception of myself as a listener or a resource person, someone who would help younger writers discover their own purposes for writing by providing space, time, and encouragement for their own learning. Where I had been foregrounding my own teaching of principles for effective writing, I began to foreground their learning of uses for writing in their own lives. It was a shift from a focus on my authority in the classroom to a focus on their authority in their worlds.

Looking back on this shift, I am aware that at the time I was not entirely certain why I was making it. The shift was not something that seemed obvious to me intellectually. As a specialist in composition and rhetoric, I knew of workshop teaching from the writings of Peter Elbow and Lucy Calkins, but I also knew that their approach was just one of many options. In fact, many other specialists considered their approach simplistic, especially when applied to college writing. In my graduate training at the University of Minnesota, I had been primarily concerned with Writing Across the Curriculum and the strategies needed for academic success. I had focused on writers like de Beaugrande, Bazerman, Bizzell, and Young, Becker, and Pike, few of whose ideas supported (or even connected with) writing workshops. When I recently read Stephen North's *The Making of Knowledge in Composition: Portrait of an Emerging Field* and saw Elbow and Calkins categorized as "practitioners" while other writers were "theorists" or "researchers" or "historians," or when I read James Berlin's topographical article ("Contemporary Composition") and saw Elbow dismissed as a Neo-Platonist while Young, Becker, and Pike were exalted as model New Rhetoricians, I recognized a clear message that, for many of the intellectual powerhouses of my profession, workshop teaching was an accepted but secondary form of teaching.

So it was not because of theory or intellectual understanding (narrowly defined) that I shifted my teaching. It was because of something else: a felt sense that my teaching methods were not allowing the learning I wanted to allow, plus a recognition that other teachers were getting more out of their students than I was. Through participation in the Nebraska Writing Project and conversations with colleagues at the University of Nebraska, I had glimpsed that workshop methods might prompt more learning (or qualitatively different learning) from what I had been able to do before. In 1986 I could not explain why I thought workshops might prompt these things, but I sensed a need to try them in my own classrooms.

Ann Berthoff reminds us (*The Making of Meaning*) that teaching practice always depends on theory, that a tacit or explicit theory of language learning always underlies our classroom behaviors. But, contrary to Berthoff, it seems to me that practice often leads theory. Because our guiding theories are so often tacit—unacknowledged, unexamined, unarticulated—our practice as teachers can sometimes move ahead of our theory. We find something "works" in our classroom (it feels right, provokes thought or interest) and so we try it again, even though we do not understand it well enough to explain why or to defend it. Our teaching practice can sometimes point our guiding theories in directions we did not know they led.

For me, shifting my classrooms to a workshop structure has functioned as just such a change in practice that moved ahead of theoretical understanding. I changed my classroom because I felt the need to, and once I began working with workshops I found that the stories of my students' experiences also changed. Instead of encountering a controlled, static process of coming to understand a small set of rhetorical principles, students began to find writing projects (and learning projects) which were far more difficult and demanding than anything I had ever posed for students before. For instance:

- Instead of arguing that his first drafts met the criteria for grades, a rigid fundamentalist young man works through five major revisions of a paper against Planned Parenthood. He struggles with tone and organization because, as a future missionary, he really wants to reach his peer small group, but ideas that seemed so clear to him alienate them.

- Instead of opting out of class because the assignments were too hard and she had done poorly in English before, a single mother begins writing a draft about her difficulties growing up in an alcoholic's family. After several attempts at this paper, she abandons it, having found an insight or voice she needed to find. In the remaining eight weeks, she produces two short stories about farm families (which she then submits to the local student literary magazine) and a term paper on tropical rain forests, which her geology professor tells her is one of the best he had received in ten years of teaching.

- Instead of writing dutiful papers and getting high marks, a self-proclaimed "good student" struggles with his writing, blocking because he discovers he does not really know *what* is important enough to him to write about. He writes in his journal all semester but finishes no papers, takes a "D" in the course, and thanks me for a class that has been a "turning point" in his life.

These stories are different from stories I could tell before trying workshops. They involve a different sort of learning from the school-and-success purpose of learning rhetorical principles. Since I have started teaching writing workshops, stories like these have convinced me that I am on to something important about learning, something we composition specialists may know in practice but have yet to understand. In the years since 1986, I have been thinking about, reading about, and participating in writing workshops (as teacher and researcher), trying to understand what the dynamics of these classes show us about learning and language.

The purpose of this book is to suggest a way of understanding the practical effectiveness of workshop classes by exploring a theory of learning which might account for it. In writing workshops, young writers are able to try out writers' roles in relation to other roles they play in their lives. Instead of restricting their behavior to student roles (learning the information or principles a teacher presents), young people in workshops can explore writers' roles as reflective thinkers, as contributors to social debate, as persuaders. It is this difference in roles that is crucial for learning. To understand this difference we need a theory of learning that allows us to focus on roles and role negotiations.

In the past few years, I have been working to understand students' stories in writing workshops as instances of identity negotiation, instances where people try to work out what their roles will be in the context of the classroom and the wider culture. In building this understanding, I have borrowed heavily from work on identity formation in social psychology, anthropology, and political theory, trying to work out how interaction in writing classrooms is like other aspects of identity formation and negotiation. I have tried to see learning to write as but one part of the larger problem of negotiating identity in a complex social world.

In many theories of identity formation, individuals are seen as having to construct their particular sense of self from the competing social definitions of self which surround them. A young woman decides to go to college, for example, only by negotiating among the self-definitions others present: the mother who wants her daughter to be a doctor; the father who believes women belong in the home; the teachers who call her a promising student; the peers who call her an apple polisher; the high school lover who wants her to stay in town; and so on. Each of these definitions of self provides opportunities for the young woman, but they also compete with each other, requiring her to negotiate her own position among them. Such negotiation forms her identity, as she understands it herself and as others attribute it to her. Identity negotiations theory examines individuals' negotiations among such competing social roles to understand how human identity operates. I have used this perspective to illuminate particular classroom problems: "underlife" in writing classes ("Underlife"), the role of imitation in learning to write ("Modeling"), leadership in small groups ("Leadership," Brooke, O'Connor, and Mirtz), and writing to an audience (*Audience Expectations*, Brooke and Hendricks).

I now believe that a theory of identity negotiations can explain learning in writing classrooms generally, in both writing workshops and other kinds of classes. In college writing classrooms, students seek (as we all do in social situations) to negotiate an identity, a version of the self, which more or less resolves the tensions they experience in that situation. Such identity negotiation always seems to go on and can explain the kind of learning that each student engages in.

The concept of identity negotiations can also explain why workshop classes "teach" different things about language than other classes do, because focusing on identity negotiations allows us to clarify the different roles involved in different classroom structures. Focusing on identity negotiations might also explain other aspects of writing education, such as why no class ever reaches all the students and how writing classes might connect with education and culture more generally.

In short, I will be arguing three ideas in this book:

1. We can best understand how and what students learn in writing classrooms by focusing on the identity negotiations which occur there. Amidst the various roles the situation offers, learners position themselves to form an identity for the self which is acceptable given the tensions of the situation. In classrooms, learning directly about the rules, principles, or processes of writing is secondary to this negotiation. Learning about writing becomes important when it operates within individuals' ongoing negotiations (with the groups that make up their classroom and culture) concerning the roles they will play and the value attached to those roles.

2. Learning to write meaningfully in our culture requires developing an understanding of the self as writer, as someone who uses writing to further personal thinking and to help solve public problems. The development of such a role, such a self-understanding, is more important than developing any set of procedural competencies. Developing such a role, however, depends crucially on connecting the role of self as writer with other roles in the culture outside the classroom, especially writers' roles in the culture at large—including roles for the self as reflective thinker and community influencer. Developing writers need to work through the tensions posed by such writers' roles in relation to school student roles.

3. Classroom practices which promote an understanding of self as writer are likely to "teach" writing more effectively than practices which focus only on expanding writing processes or on internalizing formal rules. When students leave writing classrooms feeling and articulating an understanding of themselves as writers, as people who use writing for useful social and personal purposes, they assert that they have learned something and that the course was successful. Because of the kinds of identity negotiations that occur in them, writing workshop courses like those advocated by Elbow, Calkins, Atwell, and the National Writing Project allow such a self-understanding to develop more readily than do many other courses.

These ideas, taken together, suggest a new way of looking at writing in and out of classrooms. Rather than focus directly on students' writing (whether by "writing" we mean a written product, a set of composing processes, or an understanding of the rhetorical task), I suggest that we see writing as part of a much larger and more basic activity: the development and negotiation of individual identity in a complex social environment. Like any social activity, writing does not have meaning or value in itself. Rather, human beings assign it value (for the self, for the community) when it helps them position themselves relative to one another in ways which are important to them, when it helps them understand and interact with their community.

I suggest that we try to see writing as one aspect of identity negotiation, one way that people can negotiate how they view themselves and how they want others to view them within the complex interactions of contemporary society. When we writing specialists can see writing as an aspect of identity negotiation, we will be able to see a good deal more about how and why writing education operates the way it does.

Looking at learning as identity negotiation may also help us clarify our profession's purpose in helping young people learn to write. The idea of identity negotiation seems connected to our profession's ongoing debate over what we should teach our students and what the relation of writing education to the mission of the university is. Some teachers, working in the tradition of Dewey, argue that the purpose of writing instruction is to help students develop their individual voices in writing (for example, Coles's *Plural I* and Moffett's *Active Voice*). These teachers argue that students will improve as writers and citizens by developing a better understanding of who they are and what they have to write about. In contrast, other teachers argue that writing instruction should make available to students patterns of literacy which will help them succeed as professionals and citizens in our culture (for example, Bizzell's "Arguing about Literacy" and Heath's *Ways with Words*). These teachers argue that students will lead better and more active lives when they are able to operate in and affect the culture in which they live.

In a historical survey of personal writing assignments, Robert Connors points out that this tension asks us difficult questions about the purpose of education:

> The question of personal writing is uncomfortable for many teachers because it presents such a clear mirror of one's individual philosophy of education. It is easy to feel that one's teaching is not striking the balance well between making writing meaningful to the student and making the student meaningful to the community. . . . The continuing debate, tacit and sub-channel as it may be, indicates that we as a profession have not yet come to agreement about the larger purposes of writing in this culture. ("Personal Writing Assignments" 180–181)

Contemporary discussions of writing instruction are thus circling around the issue of identity negotiations. Most teachers recognize that writing (and the way we present writing in schools) has something to do with how individuals understand themselves, that writers' roles in the culture are involved in our teaching. Our debates circle around this issue, unresolved. As teachers, we argue about what we are teaching when we teach writing, aware that our teaching has something to do with our students' experience of self ("voice") and their future place in society ("patterns of literacy").

In interviewing college writing students, I have found that they are equally aware of these tensions facing them. Individual college students need to find their own way through the tangle of self-definition and social place which writing involves. Young people need to define their own differences, find the groups from which they can gain support, and define the emergent purposes for their work. The problem facing young people is a problem of defining how "I" will act in the society "I" live in—and, secondarily, of defining whether or not some form of writing will aid in this process.

Students in first-year college writing classes, consequently, are not necessarily motivated to learn writing in itself and for itself. While some select students may be particularly interested in writing aesthetically beautiful texts or solving certain rhetorical problems because of their past experiences, most students are primarily concerned with what their performance in these college classes implies about them as college students. Do they belong in college? Are they going to be successful or not? Are the roles that a college education allows going to be roles they can adopt? These are the questions that motivate students' behavior in writing classes and their response to those classes.

Consider the following first-year student's comments about his writing class:

> *Andy:* This is only my first year, but I can remember in high school the big emphasis was on the mechanical part of writing ... and I'm wondering if other teachers are going to—other classes I take they're going to be that picky with it. 'Cause I— she hasn't been. At all. And that's what I'm just wondering if, like, this is the way it's, if it's like this all through college, fine, I think the class has helped me, but if they get in nit-picking about mechanics and everything's got to be just such a way, then that could present a problem because I don't think this class has helped in that way. And that's why I say I'm going to wait and see how it goes in other classes. (Interview, May 1986)

Andy is reflecting on the usefulness of his writing class. He has done the work assigned by the teacher and has done it successfully. But it is not his writing per se that he focuses on in responding to his class. He does not evaluate his class on the basis of the rhetorical strategies he learned or the formal features of the genres he practiced, even though his class spent a good deal of time addressing such matters as audience analysis and organization. Instead, what Andy is concerned about is what his experience means for his future success as a college student.

Andy says explicitly that he will "wait and see" what other teachers expect because there is a chance that they may not value the same aspects of writing this teacher values. In other words, he is testing what sort of behaviors are required of him as a college student and trying to evaluate what his experience means about these future requirements. For Andy, this testing involves two processes: (1) working to identify what behaviors are actually valued by the community he seeks to enter, and (2) probing himself to see whether he shares these values.

Andy is thus understanding his writing experience not in reference to a taxonomy of forms or rhetorical strategies, but in reference to social roles and social place. He is trying to define what behaviors make up the role of a successful college student and is questioning whether he can also value these behaviors. The kinds of writing his teachers teach, the kinds of writing he is asked to do to complete assignments, are looked at as symptoms of these roles, as behaviors that may be valued by those in the college community. What (and how) students like Andy learn about writing is thus a consequence of the role negotiations that take place. Writing is understood—and then rejected or engaged in—in relation to roles and values operative in the communities the student is exploring.

For first-year students like Andy, what motivates writing, what makes it significant, is its potential for finding or creating a social place, a role for the self, a relationship to social groups the individual considers important. When these people experience writing, they experience it in relation to the groups they seek to belong to and the groups they wish to exclude themselves from. Writing is a symptom of group membership ("Will writing this way make me a member of the college community?"), and writing is a means of separating themselves from groups they reject ("I'll wait and see what other teachers want").

It is this experience that I want to explore in this book. Writing's connection to social place, to identity negotiations, has, as these examples show, long functioned as a kind of unemphasized understanding in individuals' lives. Rhetoricians, teachers, and students have experienced writing as connected to social place. But all of us (especially writing researchers) have lacked a theory and a vocabulary for articulating these thoughts in anything but vague ways.

This book aims to correct this omission in our theories and vocabularies. In the next chapter, I will sketch a theory of writing as a part of identity negotiations, drawing on work from rhetoric, social psychology, and political theory which can help us explore this connection.

In the middle part of the book, I will describe the way identity negotiations influenced students and teachers in four particular classrooms. In the last chapter, I will suggest some implications that this approach has for the uses of writing in our culture and our classrooms.

2 An Overview of Identity Negotiations Theory

While shifting the structure of my writing classes, I have come to understand that the biggest difference between my earlier classes and a writers' workshop is the roles offered to participants. The most important aspect of learning to write may well be identifying and understanding what roles the self will take on as writer. Writing becomes meaningful for individuals when it supports their attempts to be certain kinds of people in their world—to be reflective adults, perhaps, or persuasive contributors to debates that concern them, or successful professionals. For students in writing workshops, the opportunity to explore writers' roles is what prompts their learning. When they can escape the notion that writing is only a means of showing a teacher what they have learned (a role James Britton once called a writer-as-examinee role), then they can begin to explore how different roles for themselves as writers might enhance other parts of their lives.

Many of the students who now complete my workshops describe their experience as just such a shift in their understanding of writers' roles. In her self-evaluation at the end of one fall 1989 course, for example, Charlotte (an entering first-year student) described a shift from a role of writer as regurgitator to a role of writer as reflective thinker:

> I feel like a writer now, not just as information regurgitator. As I look back over my process logs I see some significant changes. In the beginning I was very concerned with how others perceived my writing. "Would they laugh, smirk, or accept it?" (August 31, 1989)

> Then as time progressed, so did my writing and my attitude towards the class. Now I see myself as using writing for my own benefit to work through ideas or problems. "I needed to get these thoughts out . . . before they faded away." (November 30, 1989)

> By writing, I can clarify my opinions and ideas. C. Day Lewis said it best with, "We do not write in order to be understood, we write in order to understand." (Self-evaluation, December 1989).

Charlotte focuses on a change in self-perception, a change in what "being a writer" means to her. She describes a new stance towards writing (as a kind of clarification process) which is useful outside the course for her own benefit. What she describes is a shift to a writer's role that proves useful beyond the English classroom. For Charlotte, her learning is wrapped up in this shift.

Theories of Identity Negotiations

To understand why something seemingly as simple as a shift in roles might affect learning so powerfully, I have been exploring theories of identity formation, theories which address the way social roles influence the development of people's sense of self. The process of learning in school is a part of this larger process of identity formation. The way individuals react and relate to the different roles offered them by schools (in writing class, in physical education, in shop, during recess) undoubtedly influences how they come to understand themselves, their abilities, and their futures. Learning is influenced more by the roles offered in school than by any particular content or material being taught, because it is in negotiating a response to these roles that individuals work out their future stances towards knowledge, towards authority, and towards academic learning. A theory of identity negotiations is needed to explore and explain this crucial aspect of learning.

Such a theory would describe the way selves are formed in the interaction between available roles and individual desire. The problem of how self and society interact to form identity is a problem with a long history, and my version of identity negotiations theory emerges within a particular tradition of responses to the problem. This tradition is interdisciplinary, ranging from social psychology to anthropology and political science, and is widely accepted by researchers studying the formation of personality and social groups in various fields. Depending on the discipline, of course, this way of describing the self takes on a variety of forms. Cultural anthropologists like Clifford Geertz, for example, tend to emphasize the interpretive structures of culture in which the self emerges, while practicing therapists like R. D. Laing tend to emphasize the adaptive power of individuals in relating to the social contexts which surround them.

My version of this position is largely derived from three sources: (1) the social psychology of Erving Goffman, Erik Erikson, and R. D. Laing; (2) the political and cultural theories of educators such as Henry Giroux and Paulo Freire and feminists such as Adrienne Rich, Pamela Annas, and Mary Belenky; (3) and a tradition of interpretive anthropology described as "cultural critique" by George Marcus and Michael

Fischer. While each of these writers approaches identity from somewhat different perspectives, all of them explore how the self is formed in interaction with society, only accumulating meaning and value from such interaction.

I have chosen to call my version of this position "identity negotiations" in order to highlight two important aspects of this theory: a focus on *identity*, a term often used to denote what is most central or important about the self, but a corresponding focus on the *negotiations* which create identity, a term which denotes attempts to mitigate the clash between opposing forces, to compromise between conflicting camps, to satisfy groups with different demands. The term *identity* is most often used in psychological studies, while the term *negotiations* is taken from political and social theory. The term *identity negotiations* therefore highlights the development of the self within a complex arena of competing social forces. From such a perspective, individual identity (at any point in time) is best seen as a dynamic construct which comes into being through mitigation or compromise with the social definitions of self surrounding the individual. A person's identity arises through negotiation with the many groups which provide these definitions.

Seen from this perspective, the central tension in identity formation is a tension between social and internal understandings of the self. In any given context, a person's bearing, past, and behaviors imply that the person is a given sort of individual, but this implied identity may or may not correspond to the person's internally felt sense of self. The problem of identity formation, thus, is how to deal with this ever-present distance between implied and felt identity.

As an initial description of the differences between implied and felt identity, Erving Goffman's taxonomy of three aspects of identity is helpful. In *Stigma*, Goffman distinguishes three meanings of the word identity, each of which relates social interaction to individual experience in a unique way. The first two meanings describe implied identity, while the last describes felt identity.

First, for Goffman, identity often refers to a person's social identity— that is, the classifications of individuals that others will make on the basis of first impressions. Clothes, bearing, accent, physical attractiveness, cleanliness, and the like all come into play here. A student who attends the first day of class wearing a Delta Delta Delta sweatshirt uses this aspect of identity to be seen as a certain sort of person. Obviously, different social groups assign an individual different social identities on the basis of the same appearances. On many state college campuses, for example, students affiliated with the Greek system and students who are independents hold rather rigid stereotypic opinions about each other. On the first day of class, consequently, the Delta Delta Delta student is likely to be judged stereotypically by Greeks and independents because of the sweatshirt, and such initial judgments may affect class interaction well into the semester.

Second, Goffman identifies *personal identity* as a meaning of the term *identity*. He defines personal identity as the sum total of physical and biographical information known or attributed to an individual in a given context. Unique physical attributes—a facial deformity, for example, or great beauty—are marks of personal as well as social identity. But more important for this category are the biographical records left by an individual's journey through life. These records take two forms: the official paper trail of birth certificates, school attendance, wedding licenses, and the like; and the informal memories other people have of the individual. Different social groups value different aspects of a person's personal identity, just as they value different aspects of social identity. The student in the Delta Delta Delta sweatshirt, for example, might have a police record for driving while intoxicated during her senior year of high school, and this fact, when known by others, might raise her social standing among some elements of the undergraduate community, while it might lower her social standing in the eyes of her sorority administration.

Taken together, these two aspects of identity define the sort of implied identity that a context is likely to assign an individual. Each social context will value certain kinds of immediate appearance (social identity) and certain kinds of information about an individual's past (personal identity). Given an individual's particular social appearance and known personal history, other people in that context will tend to conceive of that person as a particular sort of person.

Goffman's third meaning for identity leads beyond the identities that situations imply to the identities that people feel themselves to have. The alignments of individuals toward the groups that surround them define what Goffman calls "ego identity" (in Erikson's sense of the person's guiding self-conception). Individuals will, Goffman points out, be perceived as a member of some groups and as an outsider in others, largely as a consequence of their social and personal identities. How persons align themselves to these groups lets others know a great deal about the self they wish to be or project. The student who wore the Delta Delta Delta sweatshirt did so to assert her membership in the Greek system as a positive and important aspect of her identity. Other students affiliated with the Greek system will project different alignments to that subculture, perhaps by dressing Greek only at Greek functions, by taking anti-Greek positions during class debates, or by never letting on to those outside the system that they are in fact members of it. By such behaviors, individuals show their alignments to the groups they seem to belong to. The particular ways individuals align themselves to such groups show a great deal about how they conceive of themselves, about their felt identity.

In fact (though Goffman does not make this point), it is this sense of ego identity formed through group affiliation that largely guides the choices individuals make about how to present their social and personal identities. How people choose to appear and behave (social identity) is a consequence of what sort of individuals they want to be classified as. Similarly, what people choose to tell about themselves (personal identity) is influenced by how they want others to understand their relationships to the groups surrounding them.

A person's ego identity thus guides the other versions of identity that Goffman identifies. The development and maintenance of an ego identity is therefore the central issue in identity negotiation. Given that the same social appearances and personal facts will imply different identities to the surrounding groups (parents, siblings, peers, teachers, employers), the central problem facing people as individuals is to negotiate their possible affiliation with these groups by how each individual manages social and personal identity. What groups do I belong to? What groups do others think I belong to? How can I influence others (and myself) to believe I am a member of the groups I want to be in and am outside the groups I only appear to be in? Or are others right, and I am actually not a member of the groups I aspire to and only a member of the groups I would like to reject?

Such questions (in some form or another, conscious or unconscious) guide self-perception and behavior, for the way an individual answers them provides motivation for public behavior and most of the tensions of private worry. An individual's psychic life can thus be thought of as endlessly concerned with social place and the negotiation of group affiliation, for from these patterns of affiliation and rejection arise the individual's sense of self. Identity thus arises in negotiation and remains a structure in flux, changing as the contexts surrounding the individual (and the individual's response to these contexts) change.

From this perspective, self-understanding at any given point in time is understood as formed through the particular history of stances the individual has taken towards the surrounding contexts. How an individual and others will understand this self at any point in time is a product of these stances. Since both the groups that surround the self and the stances the self takes towards them change over time, a person's self-understanding is not a fixed item but a dynamic force whose structure shifts and changes with contexts, groups, and stances.

This description of the self, obviously, is different from the notions of self accepted by many Americans. In our individualistic tradition, the self is often thought of as some inviolate core at the center of the organism, as a fixed consciousness that never changes, as a kind of "little me" inside that opposes the efforts of parents, peers, authorities, or other social groups to alter its basic nature. In this view, the notion of self-understanding as changeable is unthinkable: the unity and permanence of the self, or at least what is most central to the self, is held to be the essential ingredient of identity.

In contrast to this notion of an inviolate "little me," a theory of identity negotiations suggests that individuals come to experience themselves as one sort of person rather than another largely through involvement in the social situations which surround them. Whether or not there exists something inviolate in the core of the self, the self as experienced—as it comes to expression, value, and meaning—is a function of cultural interaction.

Just how directly cultural interaction determines the developing individual is an open question in theories of identity formation. Theorists seem to take a range of positions on this issue, from the almost completely culturally determinist positions of Clifford Geertz and Erving Goffman to the more psychological positions of Erik Erikson and Norman Holland. The culturally determinist version of this theory claims that the only important aspects of human identity are those which are formed in and by culture. In *The Interpretation of Cultures,* Clifford Geertz explains:

> Whatever else modern anthropology asserts—and it seems to have asserted almost everything at one time or another—it is firm in the conviction that men unmodified by the customs of particular places do not in fact exist, have never existed, and most important, could not in the very nature of the case exist. (35)

> [C]ulture provides the link between what men are intrinsically capable of becoming and what they actually, one by one, in fact become. Becoming human is becoming individual, and we become individual under the guidance of cultural patterns, historically created systems of meaning in terms of which we give form, order, point, and direction to our lives. (52)

For this position, our identity, as we experience it and understand it, comes into being through our interaction with the social patterns of our culture. In the study of identity and identity formation, this interaction is most important.

On the more psychological end of the spectrum, the emphasis is less on cultural determinism than on exploring why our lives often "feel" continuous even when in actuality there is as much (if not more) diversity as continuity in our experiences. To account for these feelings, many psychologists postulate something like the "identity themes" Norman Holland describes in *The I*—that, because of early childhood experiences, people develop certain characteristic ways of reacting to environments. While the particular meaning, value, or experience of the self will change as the environment changes, these basic ways of reacting to experience (the identity themes) remain in place, so that a person's life can be viewed the same way a piece of music is viewed: as a series of transformations and variations on a small set of enduring themes. The existence of this small set of identity themes, even though they appear in so many variations that no one instance is ever "the" identity of the person, can thus be said to account for the feeling of continuity many people experience. Such a view of identity highlights what "feels" consistent about people's lives even while recognizing the changing, interactive nature of identity. Psychologists of many sorts, for example, tend to share a focus on the individual's experience of identity, as Slugoski and Ginsburg explain:

> The paradox of personal identity—that at any moment we are the same as, yet different from, the persons we once were or ever will be—has inspired many attempts at resolution. . . . However, psychologists since William James have recognized that the problem has a distinctly psychological aspect. Here the question is one of accounting for the *experience* of continuity over time and the *sense* of unity despite diversity in conceptions of oneself. ("Ego Identity and Explanatory Speech" 36; their emphasis)

The culturally determinist position of people like Geertz and the identity theme or continuity of experience position of people like Holland represent the range of possible approaches to identity negotiation. The differences between the views are largely those of emphasis. Both views share the most important premises, that the ongoing formation of identity occurs in the history of dynamic interactions between the individual and the social groups surrounding that individual. The nature of social interactions, the individual's response to these interactions, and the individual's past history in other situations all contribute to a person's identity at any given point in time. What is important about the self in any present moment—how it acts, how it understands itself, how it feels—is formed through the history of these interactions. The self as we experience it, understand it, and act it out is a function of the dynamic interaction between individual and social groups, so to describe the self usefully we must investigate these interactions.

To summarize, identity negotiation theory rests on two assumptions about the structures of social interaction and the self:

1. Each social interaction carries with it expectations for contextually appropriate and inappropriate behavior which produce a range of roles a person might take. Each social group, however, has its own expectations for what roles its members will play in different contexts, sometimes advocating roles contextually appropriate to the situation and sometimes advocating other roles as a way of rejecting the situation's structure. Thus, whenever individuals engage in social interaction, their particular history surrounds them with expectations which delimit the range of roles they might fill in that interaction and the values of those roles for the groups that are important to them.

2. At any given point in time, our identity structure, both as we ourselves and others understand it, is composed of the conglomerate of stances we take towards the role expectations that surround us. By complying with some role expectations, we identify ourselves with various groups and their values; by resisting other roles, we separate ourselves from other groups. In any given identity structure at any given point in time, the processes of compliance and resistance are mutually important, for it is in their pattern that a unique identity emerges. To comply with or resist role expectations, moreover, we must act. Behavior thus forms a system of information by which we show our stances towards the social world. Through our behavior, we show both our intent to belong to certain social groups as well as our ability to belong.

These assumptions form the basis of identity negotiations theory. Taken together, they describe the social world as a plurality of interactions and groups (each carrying its own expectations) and identity as formed through the negotiations in which individuals work out their own stances towards those expectations.

In what remains of this chapter, I will elaborate each of these assumptions in turn, with particular emphasis on how they apply to writing classrooms.

Social Interaction and Role Expectations

Expected activity in [an] organization implies a conception of the actor and an organization can therefore be viewed as a place for

> generating assumptions about identity. . . . To engage in a partic-
> ular activity in the prescribed spirit is to accept being a particular
> kind of person who dwells in a particular kind of world. (Goffman,
> *Asylums* 186)

Individuals develop their identities in context, through interacting with
the social groups that surround them. The social contexts surrounding
individuals, however, are plural. There are many of them: a given
individual is surrounded, for example, by family, peers, schools, political
parties, religious organizations, and so on. There is no such thing as a
single, unified social context surrounding the self. Instead, each person
lives her or his life within interlapping contexts, each of which requires
different practices.

At a general level, the differences among such contexts seem obvious.
How teenagers act at home, out with friends, and at school are
remarkably different—there are clearly different practices involved. But
to distinguish among contexts is not always simple. Recently, sociologists
like Goffman (*Frame Analysis*) and conversation analysts like Craig
and Tracy (*Conversational Coherence*) have suggested that every single
interaction we take part in, from waiting for an elevator with strangers
to saying good-bye on the telephone, ought to be treated as a separate
context because the rules of acceptable behavior in each case are
distinct. Other thinkers would identify somewhat larger units of interaction as more crucial, as in Labov's studies of people's changing
patterns of speech when the groups or social classes they are talking
with change (*Language in the Inner City*). His work points out that
similar kinds of practices hold for many different interactions, changing
only when the social relationships between the speakers change.

For our purposes, it is unnecessary to distinguish where one context
begins and another ends or how big a unit of interaction a context is.
What is important for identity formation is the more general point
that each context carries with it implications about the participants. In
sociology generally, these implications are called "roles," and different
social settings are described as involving different roles for individuals.
At school, for example, a young person is assigned a "student" role,
and his behavior at school will be evaluated by others according to the
expectations of that role. Hence, by doing well at his studies he can
become a "good student," by doing poorly although trying to do well
he becomes a "bad student," by resisting work and trying to disrupt
the classroom he becomes a "discipline problem" or "disruptive student." The individual at school, in short, is able to develop any version
of the student role he wishes, but he is not free to step outside the role
altogether.

In a writing classroom, similarly, certain roles are established for participants, and individuals will respond to these roles by developing particular versions of them. As in other classrooms, one set of such roles are student roles—writing classrooms share with other classrooms some general expectations about the way people will behave as students. But more importantly for our purposes, each writing classroom will, by its activities, establish a certain role for being a writer, a certain kind of behavior that is evaluated in that classroom as writerly behavior. When we study writing classrooms from an identity negotiations perspective, one important focal point is what the class establishes as writers' roles and what versions of these roles participants develop as the class progresses.

In identity negotiations theory, it is a context's ability to delimit a range of roles for the individual that is crucial. Each context holds certain expectations for how individuals will act and evaluates the worth of individuals in relation to these expectations.

What makes these role expectations a problem for identity development, of course, is the fact that different contexts value different practices, and hence evaluate individuals differently. And contexts overlap; they are hard to keep separate. A college student sitting in class, for example, operates in a plurality of overlapping contexts. She operates as a student in a classroom, as a member of her Greek or dorm social network, as a young woman aware of potential for dating and harassment, as a representative of a particular ethnic group, and so on. Her affiliation with each of these groups produces pressures for certain behaviors in the classroom—many of which conflict. As this individual matures beyond college, she will find herself living in an even larger range of social contexts, each of which defines her roles according to different and conflicting principles.

Labov (*Language in the Inner City*) gives a striking example of such conflict related to education. Describing the lives of adolescent gang members in New York, he points out the complete disjunction between linguistic behaviors valued by peer gangs and those valued by school officials. Consequently, when boys are in classrooms filled with gang members and teachers and other students, there is no way of behaving that can please all the role expectations there. To be obedient and deferential to the teacher would assign a boy a "good student" role for school officials, but would also assign him a "lame" role for other gang members, who value creativity with insults and bravery or defiance in the face of authority. In such a situation, an individual must negotiate between roles, either choosing to reject one role and embrace another or to mitigate the conflict somehow.

Schools, of course, are not the only sites where such conflicts exist. Henry Giroux (*Theory and Resistance*), following the Frankfurt school and Paulo Freire's work, suggests that such conflict is an enduring feature of most of our institutional behavior—in school, in work establishments, in any case where values based on class, race, or sex roles interact. Laing and Esterson (*Sanity, Madness, and the Family*) show similar patterns of irresolvable role conflicts in the families of young women who later become classified as schizophrenic: the roles assigned the youngster by different family members, or by the same family members at different times, are mutually exclusive, leading to patterns of compromise that seem "mad" from our vantage point outside the family. Belenky et al. (*Women's Ways of Knowing*) show that young women frequently experience role conflict between women's normal interaction patterns in their part of our culture and the confrontational, competitive interaction patterns of good students in traditional classrooms. It would seem, then, that the role expectations of different contexts are psychologically real (we feel them; they affect our behavior) and that conflicts between such expectations are an enduring feature of social life.

Schools are particularly powerful examples of contexts in which role conflicts exist. As educational theorists like Aronowitz and Giroux (*Education under Siege*) have shown, schools in our culture are sites where competing social forces are at work. Political parties, parent groups, religious organizations, community planners, ethnic and gender advocates, youth peer groups, and others all influence what goes on in schools. All have different notions of what education should be doing and what in fact it is doing. Anyone interacting in a school setting is aware (to various degrees) of these conflicting expectations, and how individuals position themselves relative to these expectations will determine a good deal of their school behavior.

Henry Giroux has surveyed the debates on education in the last three decades and finds in traditional, liberal, and radical theorists a sort of uneasy consensus about what is involved in the analysis of schooling:

> Three important insights have emerged that are essential to a more comprehensive understanding of the schooling process:
> 1. Schools cannot be analyzed as institutions removed from the socio-economic context in which they're situated.
> 2. Schools are political sites involved in the construction and control of discourse, meaning, and subjectivities.
> 3. The commonsense values and beliefs that guide and structure classroom practice are not *a priori* universals, but social construc-

tions based on specific normative and political assumptions. (*Theory and Resistance in Education* 46)

Schools are themselves in flux. Their roles and operations are being negotiated within our culture, and a wide range of conflicting roles and expectations surround school behavior. In any school classroom, there are conflicting ideas of how individuals ought to behave, what values are operative, and what counts as success. Teachers will have their own views based on their particular educational philosophies; "successful" students will have other views, perhaps involving high grades at all costs; "marginal" students another; and individuals who do not want to be in school for whatever reason will have yet other views. Individuals will bring to school interaction a complex history of other roles they take on elsewhere (ethnic, gender, class, peer), all of which suggest views of school interaction which may not agree with any particular classroom's role for being a good student.

Any one person's experience of schooling will thus be a result of the particular way she navigates her way through these conflicting expectations. Her patterns of group acceptance and rejection will determine what kind of student (or teacher) she becomes, how she behaves, and what she values out of the experience. Any student who enters college, for example, will need to position herself relative to the groups that college represents. She becomes a "college student" rather than a member of the group of high school classmates who chose not to go on in education. She becomes an entering student who needs to prove to school officials (and herself) that she belongs and is ready for college. She needs to decide how to ignore or listen to the voices of those she knows who claim that college is elitist, only for highbrows, impractical, racist, sexist, and the like; and so on.

What goes on in writing classrooms is influenced by these cultural debates over what schooling should accomplish. Besides negotiating a stance towards the school setting itself, individuals in writing classes need also to develop a stance towards the activity of writing and what it means in the many contexts that surround them. Identity negotiations theory allows a way of describing these patterns and processes. By describing the roles that operate within a given classroom as well as how these roles connect or conflict with other roles for writers and students, identity negotiations theory can provide a portrait of the social context individuals experience within writing classrooms.

Identity as Stances: Compliance and Resistance

Without something to belong to, we have no stable self, and yet total commitment and attachment to any social unit implies a kind of selflessness. Our sense of being a person can come from being drawn into a wider social unit; our sense of selfhood can arise through the little ways in which we resist the pull. Our status is backed by the solid buildings of the world, while our sense of personal identity often resides in the cracks. (Goffman, *Asylums* 320)

If the social contexts in which we live each assign role expectations to us, and if these contexts are plural and conflicting, then the task of forming an identity within such contexts is largely a task of working out stances towards these roles. For any role, I may embrace it (doing my best to be evaluated as a "good" performer of this role), I may reject it (doing my best to avoid the role whenever possible and, when forced to take it on, to do it badly), or I may comply with it under duress (functionally doing it competently as something necessary but not central to how I see myself). I may even swing between these positions as time passes, sometimes embracing a role, sometimes merely complying with it, occasionally even rejecting it. Each of these stances (embracing, rejecting, complying) shows something about how the self relates to that role, and hence how the self conceives of itself.

The pattern of individuals' stances towards the roles they are assigned (or can be assigned) is the stuff of which identity is made. "The nature of an individual," writes Goffman, "as he himself and we impute it to him, is generated by the nature of his group affiliations" (*Stigma* 113). We understand who we are in our society by identifying the groups of people we belong to and by working out the degree of belonging we feel to these groups. The young men in Labov's study (*Language in the Inner City*) who misbehaved at school in order to gain status in the peer gang are examples of this process. By identifying with the peer gang, they distance themselves from the good student role and from the groups in their environment (other youths, teachers, perhaps some older family members) who value that role. When one of these gang members finds himself interested in a school subject or task (for example, a reading assignment in American history), he risks changing the relationship he holds to these surrounding groups—appearing less closely aligned with the gang and less far away from the values of teachers.

The structures of identity thus come about through the self's changing patterns of compliance and resistance to the social roles that are assigned the individual. The problem of identity formation is a problem of working out patterns which allow a satisfactory interaction between the roles we embrace, the roles we comply with while merely tolerating them, and the roles we reject. Any individual will, of course, be assigned some roles from all three categories by the contexts she or he inhabits, so the problem of working out a resolution is a real one. It becomes especially real because the process is not particularly conscious. Individuals are not entirely aware of the ways in which their contexts and behavior assign them social roles, nor do individuals rationally choose behaviors, roles, and contexts as they might choose between competing brands of detergent in a grocery store. Instead, many of our identity-forming actions occur at a subconscious level, in how we respond without thinking to the individuals and groups surrounding us. The ways in which we develop the patterns of compliance and resistance to social roles are thus anything but direct and accessible to conscious thought.

For Erik Erikson (*Identity: Youth and Crisis*), the problem of working out such a pattern is best understood as a subconscious search for "mutuality" amidst the threat of "crisis," as an attempt to find social groups and contexts that will reward the alignments one desires (thus functionally supporting the self one feels one "is") while holding off the uncertainty that results from having many definitions of self to consider. Erikson's oft-quoted theory of adolescent identity crisis comes about directly because of this search: adolescents, no longer comfortable accepting the narrow definitions of self offered by family interaction, are overwhelmed by the plethora of possibilities open to them and are consequently unsure how to structure their alignments into a workable pattern. They are not sure what contexts to embrace and what to reject, are not sure where to look for mutuality, and hence feel a malaise, a disintegration, that can be psychologically crippling. This situation, Erikson points out, is something each of us experiences to some degree: given the pluralistic nature of our culture, most of us have only a tentative sense of mutuality, and in moments of personal or social challenge this sense can collapse into crisis.

Given the conflicting nature of the self's assigned roles, it seems, any individual must work out patterns of alignments which in some way deal with the conflicts between those roles. Sometimes roles can be rejected as a strategy for reducing conflict—some young adults may stop going to church altogether, for example, rejecting all the implications for themselves of the religious roles they were assigned while growing up—because some roles within our culture are distinct and one can choose not to enter the contexts in which they operate. But other roles are not so easy to escape. Gender roles, race roles, work roles, for example, are part of our daily experience whether we want them to be or not. For such roles, our choices reduce to embracing the role or complying with it—and often some form of compliance is what we choose.

College writing classrooms, for those individuals who end up in them, provide such inescapable roles. Since writing classes are almost always required for college graduation, people with all sorts of experience and feelings about writing find themselves in these classes. In many ways, as Mike Rose has pointed out (*Lives on the Boundary*; "Language of Exclusion"), college writing classes thus function as a kind of initiation setting or testing ground, an environment which all must endure if they want to achieve the role of successful college student, of educated person, of college graduate. In such a setting, individuals find it hard to escape the role of student or of initiate, and their choices reduce to embracing or complying with this role if they are to remain in school.

Writers' roles in college writing classrooms, however, are not as inescapable. Writing classes, as I have argued, always promote some version of writers' roles as well as student roles, but individuals in writing classes are not under the same kind of pressure to relate to the presented roles for writers as they are to the role of student or initiate. They may have to pass a writing class in order to graduate, but they certainly do not have to like what they are doing there. College writing classrooms, hence, present participants with (at least) two very different sets of roles: student roles which they cannot escape and must embrace or comply with if they are to pass; and writers' roles which they are free to embrace, comply with, or reject as they wish. The tensions between these possible roles create a great deal of the psychic energy students expend in relating to their writing classes.

Examining how individuals create stances towards their assigned roles, especially the roles they cannot escape, is one of the main ways we understand how individuals feel about themselves. Goffman (*Asylums*) describes mere compliance with assigned roles as an essential element of the self's structure, one of the places where individuals work hardest to exhibit how they feel about themselves. In studying situations where the assigned roles for the self are very powerful (mental institutions, hospitals, schools, prisons, convents), Goffman points out that alongside the institution's role expectations there always exist well-developed patterns of underlife, patterns of behavior which show that individuals resist aspects of the assigned role, that there is more to them than this. Mental patients, for example, find ways of joking with the staff, breaking the rules, complying with the letter while not the spirit of demands, which show that they see themselves as more complex than merely mental patients.

The presence of such underlife, claims Goffman, is an essential way we deal with roles we cannot escape but which we do not embrace:

> The practice of reserving something of oneself from the clutch of an institution is . . . an essential constituent of the self. When we closely observe what goes on in a social role, a spate of sociable interaction, a social establishment—or in any other unit of social organization—embracement of the unit is not all that we see. We always find the individual employing methods to keep some distance, some elbow room, between himself and that with which others assume he should be identified. (*Asylums* 319)

Hence, in developing the patterns of alignment which form an identity, the mechanisms of underlife, of resistance to roles we must play, are as important as the more easily identified patterns of embracing and rejecting roles. The structures of identity are formed by such patterns. As we work out how we will relate to the groups surrounding us, we form an identity; when we change our alignments, we change our identity structure.

In college writing classes, the possibilities of underlife and changing identity structure are directly related to the roles for students and writers operating in each classroom. As I have argued in "Underlife and Writing Instruction," in many contemporary classrooms the roles for students and writers stand in opposition to each other. Many writing classrooms present students with writers' roles which value active and personal engagement in learning, in contrast to the passive student roles individuals may encounter in other school settings. In such classrooms, an individual's identity negotiations relative to these roles can become quite complex. Much is at stake: the individual's already negotiated role as student in the past; the individual's understanding of what an educated, successful college person is; the individual's own position towards writing and writers in the past. The ways that roles within classrooms undercut each other, the possibilities for underlife as well as compliance, and individuals' patterns of negotiations within these possibilities all determine what a given person will learn about writing in such a setting.

Identity negotiations theory requires that we describe carefully what roles are available for participants within writing classrooms and how individuals position themselves in relation to the roles made available to them. Learning, from an identity negotiations perspective, takes place in the way individuals connect and distance themselves from available roles. When people embrace the roles a situation offers and make them part of their ongoing behaviors, they have learned something. When, in contrast, they reject or merely comply with the presented roles, then they have not learned but have merely passed through the class as they daily pass through any number of contexts which hold expectations about them.

Identity negotiations theory, thus, can always describe what happens to individuals within writing classrooms (and how it happens) by locating what stances individuals take towards available roles. But the theory can also draw attention to patterns of identity transformation, patterns whereby individuals change their behaviors and their understanding of themselves. In examining writing classrooms, we therefore need to watch for what particular kinds of negotiations occur. From the descriptions which emerge, we can describe what writers' roles connect to roles students face in other contexts, and what roles impede this connection.

3 A Sequential Writing Class: Role Confusion and the Teaching of Audience

Learning, from an identity negotiations perspective, occurs when individuals are able to use new patterns of behavior to clarify or enhance roles important to them. Ideas, knowledge, and skills become important not for their own sake alone, but because they enable people to improve social relationships they care about. Learning seems less important when it is linked to roles an individual rejects or merely complies with.

Similarly, learning to write becomes important when it stems from writers' roles which enhance an individual's sense of social self. To teach writing effectively, we teachers need to create environments where writers' roles can connect directly to situations our students care about. Our students' ability to write, their motivation to write, and their effectiveness when writing in contexts beyond our classrooms all depend on students developing such writers' roles.

In the past four years, I have come to understand that exactly such development of writers' roles underlies the power of writing workshops as a teaching strategy. The primary difference between writing workshops and other classes is that the workshops allow different possibilities for role negotiation than do other kinds of writing classes. The main purpose of this chapter and the three that follow it is to describe these different possibilities from the perspective offered by identity negotiations theory. These descriptions can help us, as teachers and researchers, understand why writing workshops are so effective and the kinds of learning on which they depend.

The four courses presented in these chapters were not all writing workshops. The first two were other kinds of writing classes: an audience-based "sequence of assignments" course I taught at the University of Minnesota in 1983 and a Piagetian writing course Joy Ritchie taught at the Univeristy of Nebraska in 1986. Only the last two were workshops: Joy's 1988 course at Nebraska and my 1986 course, also at Nebraska.

The contrasts between these courses are in themselves examples of the effect of identity negotiations on learning. In the first two courses, the limitations of the roles available to students led to less learning and greater stress. My 1983 course, even though based on sound rhetorical principles, resulted in student resistance and confusion be-

cause the roles made available to students were limited and contradictory. A similar problem with limiting roles led Joy Ritchie in her 1986
course to change her curriculum midstream. By contrast, the writing
workshops presented in chapters 5 and 6 allowed students to explore
a wider range of writers' roles. In negotiating their stances towards
these roles, students identified new uses and purposes for writing and
came to see some of their other roles in a clearer light. The roles made
available to students in these four classrooms directly influenced the
kind and quality of student learning.

I present the descriptions of writing classes that follow as evidence
for (1) the greater effectiveness of workshop teaching and (2) the
explanatory power of identity negotiations theory for describing the
kind of learning upon which writing depends. The descriptions are
intended to exemplify at least the following points about identity
negotiations and writing instruction:

1. Learning to write is a function of identity negotiations first and
   content second. Even in classes dominated by content, the roles
   presented coupled with the individual's ongoing negotiations with
   these roles are what guide learning.

2. As opposed to other forms of writing instruction, writing workshops allow students to focus energy directly on writers' roles (as
   opposed to traditional student roles) and in so doing to identify
   and explore uses of writing which can function in their lives
   beyond the classroom.

3. Because students in workshops are able to explore writers' roles
   outside the narrow context of the classroom, they can begin to
   use writing as a means of addressing other roles they face
   (professional, personal, class, gender, ethnic, and so forth). By
   actively addressing the use of writing in these roles, they are able
   to enrich their understanding of them, leading to more sophis-
   ticated behavior. Such enriched understanding of other roles has
   the added consequence of allowing identification and exploration
   of various kinds of thoughtful cultural participation—an added
   benefit if the purpose of university writing instruction is to help
   individuals prepare for thoughtful participation in their culture.

In short, I present these courses in a particular order for a reason.
While identity negotiation clearly goes on in all classrooms and, I
suspect, accounts for much of the social and psychological dynamics
of any class, certain ways of structuring writing classes promote a less
stressful resolution of these processes than others do. Such less stressful

ways of conducting writing classrooms allow participants more opportunity to explore connections between writing and the rest of their lives because the problems of positioning oneself within the classroom are less acute. In presenting these courses, then, I am consciously moving from a very stressful writing classroom (in terms of identity negotiation) to progressively less stressful writing classrooms.

The courses were all studied using similar methodology, based on the case study methodology of Calkins (*Lessons from a Child*) and Graves (*Researcher Learns to Write*) and the ethnographies of Heath (*Ways with Words*) and Kantor ("Classroom Contexts"; "Research in Context," Kantor, Kirby, and Goetz). In each course, a research team (of teacher and participant-observer) attempted to gather as much data about the class as possible while it was going on, and then worked after the course was over to interpret and explain the data. Participant-observers took part in all class meetings, recording daily classroom observations and weekly reflections about the meetings. They conducted confidential interviews with the teacher and selected students several times during the semester to provide a sense of the students' changing affective and conceptual responses to the course. Both teacher and observer kept informal journals about their own reactions to the course as the term progressed. At the end of each course, the researchers collected all student work, including papers, drafts, notebooks, and student journals. After the course was over, the research team then attempted to make sense of these diverse pieces of data, seeking explanations of observed behavior and patterns in the written papers and journals.

The research team for the first class consisted of myself as teacher and John Hendricks as participant-observer. For the remaining classes, Joy Ritchie and I made up the research team, alternating positions as teacher and participant-observer in different classes. One chapter will be devoted to the description of each class. The section that follows describes a strategic writing course, which focused on teacher, audience, and evaluation.

The first course is one I taught while a graduate student in the final year of a doctoral program at the University of Minnesota. John Hendricks, a fellow graduate student and teacher, was a participant-observer in this classroom. While I have long since abandoned this particular way of teaching writing, I believe the dynamics of this course are a particularly clear example of how identity negotiations affect student learning. As I will show, this course (according to the rhetorical theory available then) should have been useful and exciting for students, but instead they found it increasingly stressful. It did not take into account the roles it was presenting for students, or how they might position themselves in relation to these roles. The result was a kind of enduring role confusion in the classroom. Students responded to this confusion by focusing more on trying to place the class relative to other courses in college (and the other expectations operating there for them as students) than on exploring the rhetorical principles they were supposed to be learning. Rather than allowing them to learn writing, the course left students worrying and confused about their roles as students in the college community.

Students and teacher found themselves frustrated in their attempts to negotiate their place in this classroom and the place of this class in the rest of their experience. This frustration can show us, as observers, a great deal about identity negotiation in ambiguous situations and about the dynamics of writing and learning within writing classrooms. How students and teacher resolved these stresses determined to a great extent what they learned, how they thought of themselves as writers, and how they responded to one another. It was through their identity negotiations, in other words, that each person's particular kind of learning emerged.

The Course

Background: The Minnesota Writing Program

This course emerged against the backdrop of the University of Minnesota's writing program as it existed between 1980 and 1985. (Since 1986, Minnesota has been engaged in significant program revision, and the developing program is now describably different.) Undergraduates entering the University of Minnesota during this period took at least two composition courses, a first-year course aimed at enhancing their writing processes, and an advanced junior-senior level course aimed at refining their writing for their major discipline. The first-year course was generic; students with all sorts of majors took it. The advanced courses were specialized for students with majors in the social sciences, the natural sciences, engineering, and business, among others.

The explicit purpose of the first-year course (as modeled in the training seminars for new teaching assistants during these years) was to make students more aware of their writing processes. The focus of the course was thus aimed more at their "prewriting and rewriting" stages than at the quality of their final drafts. Using a syllabus derived from Young, Becker, and Pike's *Rhetoric: Discovery and Change* and

Lauer and Carter's *Four Worlds of Writing*, the program invited students to explore their topics on paper by using a variety of heuristic strategies, to discuss their explorations and drafts with small groups of other students guided by the instructor, and to rework and re-explore their drafts by using a variety of revision and organization strategies. The students' final grades in the first-year course were usually based significantly on their notebooks (a sort of running journal, workbook, and rough draft recorder in which all exploration and revision took place) and on their participation in small group conferences with other students and the instructor. In evaluating the notebooks, instructors took into account the quantity of student work, the quality and complexity of their developing ideas, and the students' ability to use various tools and strategies to overcome their own particular writing problems.

Certain other elements of writing—research methods, forms for scholarly apparatus, and patterns of reasoning and argumentation— were left for the junior-senior level courses in specific disciplines. These courses focused on discipline-appropriate writing and involved heuristics for employing the concepts of the discipline, the types of writing tasks members of the discipline engage in, and any particular editing concerns and apparatus the discipline normally used.

Course Design and Teacher Rationale

The course I taught was a version of Minnesota's process-oriented first-year course, offered in the fall quarter of 1983. It departed from the program syllabus described above primarily by focusing assignments on the concept of audience. As in the first-year course modeled in the training seminar, students kept a journal or notebook in which they recorded all their prewriting through revision work, and this notebook determined a third of their grade. Students also worked with other students in small groups, and their work commenting on other students' papers also determined a third of their grade. Students were required to revise two of their papers until they were "perfect" and submit these at the end of the quarter for the final third of their grade. All of this was in keeping with the Minnesota first-year curriculum as it existed in 1983. What differed was the assignments that were given and the guidelines for evaluating them.

In this course, students were directed to write to "real" audiences outside the classroom (their bosses, consumers, students, and the like) and to design their texts for these audiences' needs. In theory, the approach was similar to Ruth Mitchell and Mary Taylor's suggestions in "The Integrating Perspective: An Audience-Response Model for

Writing" or Linda Flower's *Problem Solving Strategies for Writing*: the emphasis was on developing effective writing as defined by the imagined responses of real-world readers to whom one wrote. As teacher, my hypothesis at that time was that the form and content of effective writing vary according to the social context in which one writes, and if students could be brought to see how audiences influence the type of writing that is acceptable, then they would be more likely to produce effective writing by considering the characteristics and needs of their audiences. During an interview at the end of the semester, I explained this idea as I understood it at the time:

> Kind of the underlying assumption behind all this I guess is that the social context defines the substantive questions which define the formal characteristics of a piece, and if you approach it through that inverse pyramid you'll get to the right kind of formal characteristics almost by induction. (Excerpt from instructor interview, December 1983)

The concept underlying the course, in my mind as teacher at least, was one that focused on the relationship between text and context. If students could see that social context defines what questions readers will find interesting, and that these questions in turn help determine the structure of texts, then students should arrive at form "almost by induction." One purpose of the course, thus, was to help students arrive at an understanding of the relationship between text and context, so that they could use their understanding of context to help shape any text they had to write.

In addition to understanding the text-context relationship, a second purpose for the course was to introduce students to what I then understood as academic discourse. While teaching this course, I was hard at work on a dissertation which argued that students become socialized during their college experience to new forms of writing, talking, and thinking on the basis of the forms of language used in the academy. This dissertation used Vygotsky's theory of first language acquisition as a model and claimed that students in college progressed through the same three stages of language use as did children learning a first language (Brooke, "Writing and Commitment"). Consequently, in my teaching I tried to introduce students to what I believed were the first stages of this process by drawing their attention to academic writing. At that time, I believed that what they had experienced in high school writing was unlike anything they would experience in college writing. This belief rested on several dubious assumptions, including the assumptions that high school teachers taught only form, that college teachers universally want something different from merely formal competence, and that what college teachers want is in some ways harder to figure out than what high school teachers want. As I explained in an interview:

> Your writing that gets by the comp teacher in high school is a qualitatively different thing from the writing that gets by most of the professors here at the university. There are certainly the things that would—that we grow to write, and older people—and in some ways it's a bit of a happening to alert them to that, especially when because of the difference in task I think there is a difference in writing process. (December 1983)

If writing always depended on context (as the theory of audience argued), and if academic writing occurred in a completely different context from high school writing (as my dissertation argued), then students would need an introduction to both ideas, because the writing processes they would need in college would be qualitatively different from those they needed before.

I consequently designed this ten-week course to get students to think about how audiences influence texts and to apply this thinking to the particular audiences of academia. The course was designed in five two-week blocks. During the first week, an assignment would be given, a variety of tools would be presented which were intended to help with the assignment, and students would write a draft of their paper. On Monday of the second week, students turned in photocopies of their papers to me and to a conference group of three or four other students. Classes on Wednesday and Friday were canceled, and instead each small group would meet for an hour with me to discuss the drafts.

The writing assignments were sequenced as follows:

First Assignment: Students were told to write about the same subject for two different audiences. My example in class was writing about tax law for a New York banker and a Minnesota hunter.

Second Assignment: Students were told to analyze the way language is used in some social situation. My example in class was an analysis of how people behave during midnight screenings of the *Rocky Horror Picture Show.*

Third Assignment: Students were told to write about the same subject in three different forms, making sure each was appropriate for an audience. The forms suggested were an outline, an issue tree (Flower), and a collage (Elbow 1981). My example in class was a handout with three pieces on manic-depressive psychoses—an outline for a formal paper, a tree for a popular article, and a collage much like a short story.

Fourth Assignment: The last two assignments were aimed at what I called "academic audiences." Students were directed to think of a writing project that would be appropriate for a paper in one of their academic classes. For this assignment, they were told to write a proposal for their paper "as if they were writing it to the Independent Study Office to get credit for doing the paper." My example in class was an Independent Study form. The fifth assignment was also given at this time so that students could use the proposal as preparation for their fifth assignment.

Fifth Assignment: Students were directed to "write the paper they had proposed, appropriately for their intended audiences." My examples in class involved samples of academic writing in different fields.

All these assignments were aimed at different aspects of the text-context relationship. The sequence of assignments was intended to lead students to a better understanding of "college audiences" by the time the course was over. In an interview, I explained the ideas behind this sequence:

> So the course is designed in two parts. The first part is kind of a debugging section—that's the first six weeks—which I attempt to get them to see how task and process differs, alters, changes, based on what they're doing, what they think, what their audience is, and what the writing is supposed to look like, and such as a consequence. And once *that's* done, then we can *re-ask* them questions about writing for *college* audiences, and hopefully what we've done is to put into place some new eyes to see with—the problem adequately, so that when we say "write a humanities paper or a paper for your psychology class" or something, they will be able to focus on the right sort of issues to be able to produce that kind of paper, rather than being bound by the formal things they were taught in high school. (Excerpt from instructor interview, his emphasis, December 1983)

As I saw the course, then, the first three assignments were intended to exemplify aspects of the audience-text relationship, and the last two assignments would allow students to apply their new understanding of this relationship to the kinds of academic tasks they would be facing in the next few years. The changes I expected to see in students would be less in their writing than in how they thought about their writing, and this new way of thinking would pay off on the final two assignments.

As designed, the course had two aims. First, it aimed to get students to understand a way of looking at the text-context relationship. Second, it aimed to help students understand how to write college papers, which meant understanding how different were the demands of college from the demands of high school. It was intended to develop students' thinking about writing and to help them understand academic writing.

Classroom Dynamics

Since the course was intended to foster an understanding of audience generally and academic audiences specifically, John Hendricks (the observer) and I had expected that the dynamics of class meetings would focus on students' growing grasp of these concepts. In practice, however, an entirely unexpected aspect of the course became the dominant student concern. That concern was evaluation. In almost all interactions during the course, students found themselves worrying about how I (as teacher) would evaluate their work, and the observer and I found ourselves describing classroom interaction as dominated by questions about evaluation. As Arthur, one of the most vocal students, explained during a final interview:

> I'd say everything that I learned in here, I'm not mad I did it, you know, I think it helped me but I was so confused. I still don't know, I don't have any idea what I'm going to get in this class. (Excerpt from class interview, December 1983)

Where the course was intended to emphasize the relationship between text, context, and audience, class dynamics instead were dominated by students' questions about assignments and a concern with evaluation. This was true in all aspects of the course: class discussions during the first week of each assignment, small group meetings to discuss drafts, and individual conversations during office hours.

As intended, classroom discussions during the first week of each assignment would be spent using a variety of tools for audience analysis and a variety of tools for content development as aids in the development of the assigned papers. Conference discussions during the second week of each assignment would focus almost exclusively on how appropriate each draft was for its audience, whether it had more than one audience or no audience, and how it could become more audience-directed. Office conversations with students would not be formally scheduled, but I would be available during office hours for help as students decided they needed it.

In reality, however, a typical class unit would proceed as follows: I would enter the room before the bell on the first day of the unit and ask if there were "any questions left over from last time." Students would then almost always ask me to clarify the last assignment—just what sort of thing did I want? Could I give them an example? At the time, both teacher and observer interpreted most of these requests as questions about the form the writing should take. I would invariably respond by telling the students to "figure it out on the basis of audience," since I was interested in students' ability to produce appropriate form through considering audience needs. I would then give an example along the following lines: "If you were writing for *this* kind of audience, then you would design *this* kind of form because they have *these* sorts of needs." Students rarely seemed satisfied with these examples, however, and frequently we would spend a good fifteen minutes working through them. I consistently refused to be more specific about the form I wanted for each piece, arguing that since each student's audience would be different, each student would have to design the text in consideration of the particular audience's needs.

After discussing the assignment, the class itself would begin. I would explain how a tool for audience analysis or content development would help with this assignment, and would model the use of this tool, using a student volunteer's topic. Tools covered in the course of the quarter ranged from freewriting, to issue trees, to Aristotelian audience analysis, to Young, Becker, and Pike's tagmemic matrix. The class usually became engrossed in these exercises, and the class period would usually end while the class was still involved in the application of the tool to the volunteer's topic. I would then summarize the main points of application as the bell sounded. Following class, I would privately answer questions from four or five students (usually more requests for clarification of the assignment, or for how today's tool would apply to their topics).

During the second, or conference, week of each assignment, students would bring copies of their papers for their conference groups on Monday, and I would meet separately with each group on Wednesday and Friday. In conference, students discussed each paper in turn, having read them beforehand outside of class. I would focus discussion on how well the paper would meet the needs of its audience, and ideas for revision were based on improving the audience's reaction, on narrowing the audience, or on finding an audience for the ideas. During these conferences, students often mentioned "understanding better" what they should have done with the assignments and feelings of being "surprised" because they thought I had wanted something else. Students would leave conference groups to revise their work before turning it in again the next Monday; and the sequence of modeling tools in class, then conferencing in small groups, would repeat.

Even given the amount of discussion and modeling of the assignments during each two-week unit, students still found themselves unsure about what they were supposed to do. As they dealt with their uncertainty, they found themselves forming different understandings of what I was up to. Arthur summarized the feelings of several students about this uncertainty, pointing to the ways it held them back:

> I still think it might have been better on some of the papers if I had a better idea what the assignment was—maybe not what I had to do with it, but what it was.... Because that was kind of procrastinated for a week before I got started because I couldn't figure it out. (Excerpt from final interview, December 1983)

Other students, in contrast, found this uncertainty a productive element of the course, as Lars explained:

> I think a lot of the course was finding out on yourself and that's why he seemed vague a lot of the time. You know, he was trying to teach you by letting you figure it out yourself. Doesn't tell you a lot, the assignments seem vague, and then you do it and you find out about [inaudible]. And that's his method of teaching which I think worked for me. (Excerpt from final interview, December 1983)

This overall uncertainty about assignments and evaluation led to a fairly constant stream of students coming to me for extra help during office hours. Several of these students came to discuss drafts and revisions of assignments. (Because final grading was based partly on two pieces students had revised further after conferences, revisions were important.) Others came to get additional clarification about assignments or about grading. These individual conversations helped particular students feel a bit more comfortable with their work, but did not quell the overriding concern they had with evaluation, as Jeremy explained:

> When I talked with him he said he'd rather grade on improvement than he would on your work.... If he really does good on you he'll look at how you started writing, then he'll look at your final papers, and he'll grade on that purpose, but no one's sure how he's going to do that. I mean he says he is, but that doesn't mean he is, I mean you really don't know exactly what he's going to do. (Excerpt from final interview, December 1983)

Class dynamics, in other words, were very different in practice than I had expected when I designed the course. Besides focusing on understanding audience analysis and academic audiences, the course also developed an enduring focus on my own expectations for their work—on my expectations for their papers, their thinking, their behavior as students in my class.

Classroom Roles for Student Writers

When John Hendricks and I began trying to make sense of this class's dynamics, we were immediately confronted with a problem. How could we account for the unexpected emphasis on teacher expectations and evaluation, since we had expected an emphasis on understanding audience?

The reason for this unpredicted emphasis was not immediately apparent as long as we thought about it in terms of the concept of audience, because most students reported that the emphasis on audience was helpful. Nor could we account for it by focusing on the actual grades I assigned, because the grades were similar to those given in other courses and in most cases showed a progression from "C" to "B" or "A" levels as the course went on. When we thought about this emphasis in terms of the identity negotiations the classroom allowed, however, some good reasons for it became clear. This classroom was an extremely confusing place for negotiating a coherent sense of self, because the roles it provided individuals were extremely contorted and the social relationships between individuals (especially between teacher and student) kept shifting.

Any classroom assigns the same individual different roles on the basis of the different groups which interact there. Stereotypically, compliance with the teacher's demands results in being assigned a "good student" role by the teacher, a "smart person" role by those students who also comply, and a "teacher's pet," "nerd," or "earhole" role by those students who resist compliance. At the same time, other aspects of a student's behavior—for example, a male student's ability to make occasional wisecracks which other students can hear but the teacher can't—will help assign the individual a role in peer interaction (for example, a "bad ass" role by other males or perhaps a "cute guy" role from some females). Any classroom is filled with such diverse and competing ways of assigning roles, and individuals thus negotiate their own identity within the classroom by acting in ways which show their stances towards each of these roles.

In my classroom, for example, one student wore his Navy uniform to class frequently and made lots of wisecracks while I was writing on the board. Some students laughed at his antics, and others acted disgusted by them. Such behaviors were used by all involved as underlife behaviors always are—to show there are other ways of understanding these people, other aspects to their selves, than the official interactions of the classroom can allow (Brooke, "Underlife").

But my course also produced a different sort of tension, a tension centered directly in the teacher-student relationship. Students had to work through several conflicting ways of understanding this relationship, all of which operated at the same time. Since my behavior as teacher supported parts of each of these different ways of seeing the relationship, students found themselves unsure about the real expectations for their behavior as students and thus were unsure how to negotiate the kind of "identity" they wished to be assigned.

My course produced at least the following three ways of understanding the teacher-student relationship:

1. *"Teacher is evaluator; student is performer."* A particularly dominant aspect of my course supported the notion that teacher and students were operating within a traditional classroom structure where teachers give assignments, students do them, and teachers evaluate how well they did them according to some criteria, explicit or inexplicit. Much of my behavior fit into this relationship. I assigned fairly specific writing tasks for students, I required all classroom tools to be tried at least once in the notebooks, I graded each draft of students' papers, and I did not write my own papers along with the students (thus highlighting my position as evaluator instead of participant). All of these behaviors define the context for evaluating the course as that of a stereotypical classroom.

The student-teacher roles created by these behaviors were reasonably familiar to students. The teacher role became, in this relationship, that of someone who knew certain material (in this case, the needs of audiences, specifically college audiences) and gave assignments intended to let students demonstrate that they also knew this material. The student role became that of someone who merely learns a given body of material and then demonstrates this knowledge in a test-taking setting. In such a relationship, each teacher-student interaction would be seen as evaluative. Each draft of each paper and each time the notebooks were turned in would be seen as testing opportunities for students to demonstrate their knowledge. Their overall success as students in the course would be measured by the combination of results in these various testing opportunities. It was this testing aspect of the teacher-student relationship that caused many students to worry so much about getting the assignments right, because in this relationship always doing the assignments wrong meant you were doing very badly as a student. Laura explained the frustrations caused by this way of seeing the course:

> I would get so frustrated. . . . [My first draft] was so off what he wanted you to do, you know, that I wouldn't get a good grade,

then I felt bad. You could just get yourself in a hole and said, "Well, you know, if I'm never going to do the assignment right I'm not going to bother putting any effort into it." (Excerpt from final interview, December 1983)

2. *"Diagnostician to developing adolescent."* A second aspect of my course was a relationship between teacher and student very much like that between a diagnostician and a developing adolescent, a relationship reasonably distinct from the stereotypical "testing" relationship. I gave two grades on each paper, one of which was for "how well you got the point of the assignment," the other for "how I would grade the paper if it were submitted as is as part of the final portfolio." I guided discussions in small groups to ways of thinking about "audience" and "texts." I emphasized the notebook, the "process," as much as if not more than the "product," and told students I would evaluate the notebook on the basis of "how it showed the progress of your thinking." Finally, I structured the assignments in the course as a "progression of exercises leading to a better understanding of audience." All of these aspects of my behavior suggested that I, as an older and more educated adult, knew things about thinking and mental development which the students did not, and that I was diagnosing and monitoring the course of their individual mental development as the quarter progressed.

Such a relationship shifted the simple test-taking context of "student as performer, teacher as evaluator" into something quite different. While still being assumed to know certain material the students do not, the teacher in this relationship takes on a dual role. One part of this role is evaluative and involves looking at the overall change or development in the student over the course of the semester as evidence of growth. The second part of the role is facilitative and involves sequencing tasks for the students so that they are more likely to progress in the desired skills. Consequently, the student role shifts from that of someone who merely demonstrates competency on straightforward tests to that of someone who needs to change in more global ways during the course. Success as a student, in this model, comes less from specific exercises than from the overall progress or development exhibited during the quarter. Students emphasized this relationship when they pointed to my grading on overall improvement, and many students recognized that the particular kind of improvement I was looking for had to do with understanding audience and college:

> *Lars:* I think he really just wanted improvement in each of us, I mean, I don't think he wanted any particular kind of writing as long as we improved.
>
> *Interviewer:* What do you mean by "improve"?

> *Lars:* That, you know, to be writing like he said for a college level audience. Be concerned about your audience, be writing in a different style for college. (Excerpt from final interview, December 1983)

Students, in other words, understood me to have an agenda for their improvement in the course as a whole, perhaps an agenda in contrast to my specific desires for any particular assignment.

Both this aspect of the teacher-student relationship and the first aspect, however, share a common assumption that the student role primarily involves demonstrating to the teacher some kind of knowledge the teacher already has. Whether this is knowledge the students demonstrate in particular tests or by an overall development in thinking skills, the teacher in some sense owns and defines this knowledge, and a good student is someone who comes to understand and demonstrate this knowledge too.

3. *"We're all writers, helping each other."* The third aspect of the teacher-student relationship is of an entirely different kind, one between an older and more experienced writer and younger writers. From this perspective, the class became a place where writers with different purposes and audiences met to share what they were working on and to help each other with it. The conference group meetings, the acceptance of nonacademic texts like posters and pamphlets as final writings, and the use of student volunteers' real topics for class exploration all supported this understanding of the course. This relationship, if carried to logical conclusion, would create roles for students as people who choose their own topics and audiences for their work, and a role for the teacher as a sort of elder craftsman who helps them overcome the problems they face. But in this class, this relationship was submerged in the overwhelming evaluative relationships sketched above. Working against this role were the facts that I set all the assignments, that I graded each draft, and that I had a specific set of ideas about audience and academic writing which students were supposed to learn. While aspects of this writer-to-writer relationship existed, they were so submerged in the more dominant teacher-to-student roles that students only perceived them as vagueness or as a problem with the course, as Carol makes clear:

> I think he was meaning—a problem that the class was more for people who are having problems with their writing and for people who need to get taught notebooks, and that maybe . . . , if it was fine, then he thought it was great, but he also wanted to see that you do a lot of work, that you are really working, learning anything

about how to write. More for people who are having problems.
(Excerpt from final interview, December 1983)

Student responses to the class—especially their frustrations—can be understood in relation to the complex nature of the teacher-student relationships in this class. Each student somehow had to come to grips with me and what I was teaching, and this meant negotiating, from the conflicting messages I was sending, an understanding of what I was up to. My course, in other words, confronted students with a problem for identity negotiation in the classroom: how they were to understand themselves and their behavior depended on how they understood the "expectations" operating in this class, but the expectations were unclear because the teacher-student relationship was a mess of multiple and competing possibilities.

I will present several representative student responses in the next section. These responses show the power and complexity of identity negotiation as a process in classrooms, for individual students had to find a way of resolving these tensions in the classroom in terms which supported the sort of self they felt themselves to be. The nature of individual students' learning is largely a product of this process, for the way they understood what they had learned is related to the sense of self they were able to work out amid the possibilities the course offered.

Identity Negotiations in One Small Group

In this class, four or five students worked together throughout the quarter in conference groups. These groups read and commented on each other's writings, met together with me apart from the rest of the class, and frequently worked with each other outside of class. The observer took part in two of these small groups throughout the quarter. To clarify the nature of identity negotiation in response to this course, I will discuss in detail one of these groups.

The most representative group we studied was comprised of four students, two female (Susan and Kris) and two male (George and Doug). These four students interacted well throughout the quarter, but varied tremendously in their responses to the course and their strategies for dealing with its demands. In my opinion, all four dealt successfully with the course, if we view it from their perspective, and all four had responses to the course which were representative of other students. The stances these students took towards the course show the various ways individual students judged their experience and negotiated an identity for themselves as students and writers in relation to this experience.

Doug

By traditional standards, Doug was the least successful student in this group. At midterm, he was failing the class, but he managed to pull a "D" by the end. Doug, however, did not resent or dislike his position as marginal student—he was always pleasant to me and the other students and basically claimed to "understand" the class. By his own admission, he was not very interested in writing. In the first week of the quarter, he evaluated his typical writing process partly as follows:

> How I feel about writing in general, is that I dislike it. That is not to say that I don't always dislike it, but seventy-five percent of the time, I don't look forward to it. (Student journal entry)

Doug went on to say that he usually wrote a five-page paper in about three hours, claiming that "in that time I should be able to say all the things I want to, but sometimes quality is lacking." He listed invention problems ("I need questions to ask that I can't think of myself, to ask") and procrastination as his biggest writing problems.

Throughout the course, Doug wrote comparatively short papers, averaging one or two pages when other students wrote five to ten. He claimed to "sit and think" a lot, though his notebook-journal remained relatively empty. When he turned in his journal on the last day, he had the following note attached to it:

> Robert,
>
> I didn't finish my last two drafts because I don't think it would make any difference in my final grade. I guess that is a terrible attitude to have, but I just can't shake it. Every time I sit down to write tagmemics and audience analysis I draw a blank, and the only way I can finish the assignment is by just doing a draft. Taking the class over again will probably be the best thing for me to do since my GPA will be dragged down the tubes if I let it stand as is. I'm sorry if this disappoints you, but I guess Comp isn't my bag.
> Sincerely, Doug.

Doug, in short, functionally resisted any of the course's possible roles for being a good student. He did not feel that the amount of work required for the class was worth his time, whether he understood the teacher-student relationship as focused on separate testing units in each assignment or on overall mental development. He was willing to be labeled a bad student—even a failing student—and instead to take the course over with a different instructor.

For Doug, what justified this rejection of student roles was his recognition of a writer's role he saw operating in the course. Doug explained that he thought the course was not a normal first-year composition course, but more like a course "for people who wanted a writing career." This did not particularly bother him, he said, it "just wasn't his thing." The reason it wasn't his thing was that his experience in other classes suggested to him that he could do just fine as a college student without all the work I required for papers in my class. As he explained:

> I had to write an *essay* for another class, and I just read the information I needed to know for that essay, and I wrote down the stuff for the professor, and I got an "A" on the paper. Now, if I would have done that for this class, I probably would have got a "D" on the notebook and a "D" on the paper, you know. I guess if that's two different things he wants, I guess. I mean, he wants—my *other* professor wanted—I don't know, I guess I was doing all right *without* the stuff. (Small group interview, December 1983)

Because he was doing all right in other courses without all the stuff I was demanding, Doug felt he could safely reject my class as unnecessary. He chose to separate himself from the course, claiming that his ideas and mine were both valid, just different: this was a course for writers, he had no intention of being a writer, therefore his poor standing in the course was not a problem.

Apparently, Doug understood writers to be people very unlike himself, people who wanted to accomplish more with their writing than simply doing well in college. Although he did not explicitly describe his view of writers in our interviews, such a perspective would explain why he supported his classmate George's positive evaluation of the course when my ideas were being attacked by the two women in his small group:

> *Doug:* I don't think it's *his* way as much as it's the way it should be done, you know.
>
> *Interviewer:* What do you mean by that, Doug?
>
> *Doug:* I mean that it's *not* his personal view, it's how he thinks, it's how he *interprets*, what the right way of writing *should* be done, instead of, it's *not* something that it's his *personal* view. (Small group interview, December 1983)

Because he never intended to be a writer, it did not matter that he was doing poorly. He could say that my ideas were fine for writers and that composition was not his bag. In his mind, my goals and his own goals were both valid, just different.

Doug thus found a way of understanding his relationship to the course which made his lack of success in the classroom acceptable. His version of me implied a teacher who was an authority on writing and could therefore be trusted if one wanted to be a writer (which he didn't). Doug accepted, in short, my relationship to students as "a more experienced writer" and "diagnostician"—he accepted that I knew more than students did about "how writing should be done" and that I really intended to help students write more effectively.

His understanding cast us in a separate but equal relationship—we understood each other, even respected each other, but chose to disagree about the importance of being a writer. Such a stance meant, of course, that Doug did belong in college, could think as well as I could, and just needed a different course to fulfill his writing requirement. It was a way of understanding his experience which protected his identity as someone who belongs in college.

Susan

Unlike Doug, Susan had high expectations for the course and found herself frustrated by her experience. In her initial self-evaluation, Susan explained that she intended to get a Ph.D. in child psychology and that her goal for her freshman year was to make the dean's list. She went on to describe her typical writing experience:

> When I am writing I like to get all the main ideas out and use my creativity. This results in somewhat of a mess because my mechanics and punctuation are awful. I have always done well in english because of my style and imagination but when it came down to the mechanics I have always needed a great deal of help. . . . It is frustrating for me to get back a paper that says "excellent work." Susan but then read further and see in red ink, need's work on punctuation and format. It doesn't come easy for me. But I am more determined then ever to succeed. (Unedited student text)

By her own admission, Susan entered the course with high motivation to succeed in college and more mechanical difficulty than the average Minnesota freshman. By the time she left the course, she had become successful in writing papers in my course, but had also become dissatisfied with the whole experience, being relatively sure that I was idiosyncratic and she was not learning anything useful.

In light of Susan's experience in the class, her response was not extreme. Of the four students in her small group, Susan was the only one to be sent to the Writing Lab for extra help with her mechanics. Her experience with her tutor in the Writing Lab highlighted in her mind the unusual nature of the course. During her third meeting with her tutor, she found out that he did not understand the assignment either, never having heard of issue trees and collages as exploration devices. At a meeting that Susan arranged with both me and the tutor, we agreed that I would tutor her since the tutor had not worked with these tools before. As Susan described it, from that point on she got high marks on her papers, "but then *he* wrote my papers."

In the taped interview with her group, she described her strategy as "giving the teacher what he wants" for the purposes of a grade, but explained that she would abandon this style of writing as soon as the course was over:

> He tells me how to do them, I do them exactly the way he wants them, I'm getting good grades, but that isn't the way I'd write my papers, so I don't—I'm afraid that—I don't know what's going to happen when I get *out* of the class, because I won't keep writing my papers the way *he* wants them. (Small group interview, December 1983)

Although Susan worried about whether my expectations would transfer to other college classes ("I don't know what's going to happen . . ."), she had pretty well decided that I was an anomaly and did not need to be taken seriously. As she described it, "Only *he* knows what he wants":

> Well he—he knows exactly what he wants to see, and if he doesn't see it, he's like a little *kid* and you're the one that suffers. (Small group interview, December 1983)

Susan thus produced a judgment of the course that protected her sense of self as "motivated student" in the face of negative response. Where Doug could separate himself entirely from the class because he did not want to succeed at what was offered, Susan was deeply challenged because she wanted very much to succeed as a writer and college person. Her response to her experience with the class defended this sense of self—she decided that I was "not typical" of college people, and that her experience here did not count. I was odd, so her lack of success did not reflect on her ability—it reflected on me. Susan spent a great deal of time during the taped interview, for example, complaining about how different this course was from those her peers had. She was frustrated because she felt I was "hiding" my specific requirements from the class throughout the course.

Her overall response to the course, then, was to experience the concept of audience as the direct individual evaluating one's writing (in this case, her teacher) and to experience my particular evaluations as odd, atypical, and useless for her future life as a college person. She did not buy, in other words, the teacher-students relationship of "a more experienced writer" or "diagnostician." Like any teacher, I was just an authority who demanded that students perform tasks and then evaluated those tasks according to some criteria I had. As a teacher, I was lousy because I did not make my criteria clear. For Susan, this was the "reality" of her experience; the rest was gravy.

Like Doug, Susan thus negotiated a stance towards the class which supported her sense of self. Like Doug, she chose to place herself outside the roles developed in the class, and, like Doug, she took this stance in order to preserve a positive sense of self in the face of negative feedback. Unlike Doug, however, she could not see me as an authority about writing at all. For her to maintain her sense of herself as a successful student who was going to be a successful academic, I had to be seen as merely an arbitrary authority, as an aberration from other college people, as an example of a poor teacher. Her learning was thus completely colored by her need to protect her conception of herself— she left rejecting the course entirely, both teacher and ideas, because this stance toward the course allowed her to maintain her conceptions of self in the face of negative feedback.

George

The story of George's progress through the course is the story of a sea-change. At first, George was extremely frustrated, but by the end of the quarter he had become the foremost defender of my ideas. He was able, we think, to join together his writing practice with the concept of audience that the course presented, and consequently found a strong sense of identity as "good student and writer."

For the first four weeks, George was the most vocal and seemingly most frustrated member of the class. He repeatedly grilled me for more explicit instructions during class, after class, and during office hours. He got lower marks than he wanted on his papers, and consistently asked for clarification of "What You Want." Then, suddenly, in the middle of the fifth week, George changed. He started getting good grades (at one point, I told him he had written "the best paper in the class"), began to help explain assignments to other students, and began to act relatively happy in class. When John Hendricks asked his group to give their responses to the class, he was the first to volunteer, and it was exactly on this change that he focused:

I like it. *Now*. But it was really confusing at first, I didn't like it at all. Then once I saw what he was trying to do and stuff, makes sense. Makes more sense than other teachers who just concentrate on spelling and stuff like that. He concentrates on what's in your writing not on spelling and stuff like that—audience and stuff like—'Cause you can use that when you get out of that class, you have to write to a certain audience and stuff, you know how to write to an audience. (Small group interview, December 1983)

For George, the change in his response to the class was in part due to an entirely new conceptualization of the course. He began, it seems, understanding the course very much as Susan had, as a response to a single teacher with specific requirements (teacher as tester). What changed is that midway through the course George understood the concept of audience as I was trying to explain it and suddenly saw the course as one example of how readership influences writing. He could then accept a relationship to me as "more experienced writer" because he now understood how to do the tasks before him. He could also accept a relationship to me as "diagnostician" because he now felt he had advanced in his thinking about writing.

The experience in this course taught George something generalizable, something he would be able to use in other courses and other writing situations, and this experience meant he was a success as a college student and writer. George felt he had worked hard for his insight, that he found it tremendously useful, and that he was frustrated with the way Susan and Kris were responding to the course. His repeated defenses of his experience seemed an attempt to prove that his understanding of audience was insightful, that he was "developing," and that I was not "just weird" as Susan was arguing. In the most remarkable incident on tape, close to the end of the interview George suddenly turned to the interviewer and asked:

> *George:* Is [Robert] working for his doctorate?
>
> *Interviewer:* Yup. He's in the midst of writing his dissertation.
>
> *George:* So he's just about a professor, huh?
>
> *Susan:* God help us all.
>
> *George:* [to Susan and Kris] *See!*
>
> *Kris:* Hanhh! [gasp]

George, here, seemed to be seeking for some kind of outside verification of his experience, some kind of outside support for his sense that this was a good class. In the series of questions and comments that followed, he pushed for more and more information about me and used the information he got to support his opinions with a quiet but forceful

"See" directed towards his skeptic peers. It had become very important to George to prove that I knew what I was talking about, because he wanted to hold on to his sense of his own development in the course:

Interviewer: "See!" What do you mean, "See!"?

George: He probably knows how—he probably knows how to write more than you do.

Doug: Yeah, of *course* he does—

Susan: Yeah, but he knows how to write the way he wants to write, but the way he was taught to write—

George: [to interviewer] What do *you* think of him as a writer?

Susan: I was not taught to write that way.

Kris: He—he's teaching us—

Interviewer: What do I think of him as a writer?

George: Yeah.

Interviewer: [pause] Well, I—

Susan: [chuckles]

Interviewer: I've read some of his finished work, and I think that it's extremely lucid, very insightful, he's a very—

George: Hunh!

Interviewer: —able writer, *I* think. For audiences like me.

George: For audiences like the other *college* people?

Interviewer: Yeah. I mean, . . . I would be an academic audience, and the writing that I've seen of his for that audience. I've seen, for example, a number of the chapters from Robert's dissertation.

George: What is a dissertation, a *book?*

Interviewer: [coughs] Basically.

George: On how to *write,* or what?

Interviewer: Ph.D. dissertations are concentrated in-depth studies in specific areas of interest. It's a way to demonstrate academically that you have control of a subject in depth, and Robert's is on composition *theory,* theories of how people produce written discourse.

George: Is he using the ideas in his dissertation on us?

Interviewer: Uh, I think that, that, *I* see, from what I've read of his stuff, *yes*—

George: [to other students] See.

Throughout this passage, George pushes the interviewer for information that will prove I know what I'm talking about. He pushes to find out (1) that I am an able writer, (2) that college people like my writing, (3) that I am writing a "book" on writing, and (4) that the ideas in this "book" are being taught in my classroom. This chain of information is all aimed at establishing that I know what I am doing so that George's sense of the class and his experience can be confirmed. To maintain his sense of himself as someone who "learned" in this classroom, he needed to establish me as a real authority on writing (teacher as diagnostician) because then his own success in the classroom established him as someone who "developed more than others."

George's reactions and questions served to position himself in relation to teacher, observer, his peers, and "college people" in ways which increased his sense of self-importance. Although the negotiations he used to achieve this end were radically different from Susan's or Doug's, he too experienced the course in ways which allowed him to work out an acceptable, positive sense of self in this environment.

Kris

Kris's experience of the course is most typical of the class as a whole. Her reaction was decidedly ambivalent—she saw the point to much of what happened, but felt completely frustrated much of the time. Hence her sense that she was learning, but that something was wrong:

> *Kris:* I'm not saying that what he's teaching is bad at all, I mean I—
> *George:* Just the way he's doing it?
> *Kris:* Yeah.

In her initial self-evaluation, Kris described herself as someone who loves to write, whose father is an author, and who had done well in advanced placement English her senior year of high school. For these reasons, she was sure composition was going to be her easiest class. As the course progressed, however, Kris found herself more and more frustrated because she could not seem to get the grades she wanted, and she felt more and more that she could not get those grades because she could not get inside my head to see what I wanted. This made her response to the course completely ambivalent. Like George, she liked many of the ideas in the course; like Susan, she thought I was idiosyncratic and dictatorial:

> I don't like—I mean I like—the, like George said, the things that he did were great, working with audience and stuff like that, and, you know, *not* just working with spelling, but I just don't like the way he grades at all—because I think that if you don't do exactly what he had in mind, that he'll give you a bad grade.

As the course progressed, Kris's frustration with not getting high grades made it harder and harder for her to like the course and easier and easier for her to reject it as odd. During the group interview, Kris consequently seemed like a tennis ball, bouncing between George and Susan, agreeing with one, then agreeing with the other, not seeming to notice herself-contradiction. Like George, she wanted to claim she had learned something; like Susan, she wanted to claim she was a "good student" in the face of negative feedback from her teacher. Hence the contradiction. She wanted both identities, the identity of successful learner and the identity of good student, and her experience in the course put these self-conceptions into conflict.

Consider the contradiction involved in the following two excerpts:

> *George:* I mean, you know how to evaluate the audience, you know how to write for them, you know what they want—
>
> *Kris:* In your way of—I think that's important.
>
> *George:* You know, how to find out what they want and stuff like that. I *never* did *that* before.
>
> *Kris:* Well, 'cause my dad—I know that's true because my dad's, he writes a, he's an editor of a newspaper and he writes an article for the weekend. He, you know, he just—*he has to be* aware of who he's writing to, and I mean it's *true.* He's *not* just writing to a teacher, he's writing to, you know, whoever's going to read the paper.
>
> *Susan:* Then how are you, you know, how are you going to know if we been doing it right, because he's so—
>
> *Kris:* I know, but, you know, other classes maybe you only have to write one paper, so, you're just going to have to *do* it however, you know, and *Robert* is just trying to teach us to write, you know, *his* way, but maybe other teachers aren't going to like that so you should just—he should *help* you figure out what *you* want to write. (Small group interview, December 1983)

In the first excerpt, Kris pretty much agrees with George that "audience" is a true and useful concept; in the second, she pretty much agrees with Susan that I was teaching *my* way to write, and it probably was not anybody else's way to write. Kris sits on the fence, sure only that she is frustrated, with a whirl of audience- and identity-related items swirling around in her head—evaluate the audience, find a readership, please the teacher, what does he want, why did I get "C," who is my audience and what will Robert think of this, does his opinion even count, why is he so weird, I know I'm a goodwriter—why doesn't he see it? To claim that Kris understood what I was trying to teach, or to claim that she did not, would be to miss half her experience—she experienced the full confusion that results from the coming together of the teacher-student relationships in this classroom. The result may be learning, since George, Doug, and Kris all claimed they learned, but the result is certainly frustration and tension, which each student exhibited in a different way.

The way the individual students came to understand the course's tensions thus produced a different view of the value of the course and their own identities in relation to it. Some students, like Doug, separated themselves completely from the course, refusing to let what happened there implicate them at all. Others, like George and Susan, took a strong stance towards the course, thereby defending their own sense of themselves as students, writers, and learners. Still others, like Kris, found themselves taking several stances towards the course, being finally unsure whether their experience in it was valid and whether they were better writers or poorer students as a consequence. For all of these students, their identities were changed or threatened in some way by their experience, and the stance they took towards the course significantly reflected the sense of self they wanted to preserve.

Identity, Classroom Roles, and Learning

This description of students' experience in one writing class illustrates three important points:

1. Learning is profoundly affected by identity negotiations, even in courses focused on content or principles.
2. The roles available in a classroom like this one limit learning by restricting students' identity negotiations to a narrow range of roles.
3. These limitations are clearly a problem for writing instruction, exemplifying a need for a different kind of classroom structure.

My course was designed to teach strategies of writing by focusing on audience analysis. What students learned, though, had much more to do with the identity negotiations they became involved in during the quarter. What they learned depended on the kind of person they wanted to be and the distance between this person and the person that classroom interaction implied they were.

What students learn from classes like this one is not only a consequence of presented information or performed tasks. Learning is also a consequence of identity negotiation. Students leave courses with a sense of how their learning connects with aspects of their identities, and it is these connections which define how their learning will be used in the future.

Too often, we teachers evaluate learning only by performance, by how well students "do" in our classes, without looking at how classroom interaction connects (or does not connect) with students' senses of self. By looking only at performance, we thus obscure our understanding of much of their real learning.

Susan and Doug are both examples of this point. By performance standards, Susan learned a great deal from this course. She got a "B" at the end of the course, a grade that is usually taken to mean she did all the work that was required and did it well. The grade suggests she must have learned the material that was presented. This view of her learning, however, ignores the ways in which she connected the course to her developing sense of self. For Susan, there was no connection. The course existed only to be endured and rejected as soon as it was over. She will "never write that way again." She did not learn what the course set out to teach, even though she earned a "B"; instead, she learned that teachers are arbitrary authorities who are often unclear and petty in their evaluations.

Similarly, what Doug's performance might imply is out of step with how he experienced his classroom learning. By performance standards, Doug apparently learned very little. He got a "D" out of the class, a grade which is usually taken to mean he did some of the required work but not enough to show any real attention to the material. Yet he could articulate an understanding of audience and of "being a writer" similar to the understandings I designed the course to teach. Doug simply rejected the idea that this version of "being a writer" applied to him. It is not easy to say what Doug learned or did not learn in the context of such identity negotiations.

For these students, learning in this writing class is therefore best described by their particular identity negotiations. George learned that he was well on his way to success in college and had surpassed his peers. Susan learned that teachers are arbitrary authorities, and hence she needed to be more careful about which courses she would take. Doug learned that professional writers think and behave in certain ways that he does not and that a person can succeed as a student without becoming such a writer. Kris learned that she was frustrated, that teachers might say things she agreed with and then grade her down because she cannot read their minds. For these individual students, what stands out most about their course has to do with their identity negotiations, with their felt positions relative to groups like "college people," "students," and their peers.

Did these students learn anything about writing per se? The answer to this question is very hard to evaluate. In one sense, they did learn something—most students mentioned audience as a concept they had learned from this class and thought (in various ways) that the concept might help them accomplish writing tasks in the future. In this sense, yes, they did learn something about writing.

In another sense, though, what these students learned had more to do with their own positions relative to college people, relative to teachers, academics, and other students. The students' identity negotiations focused on their relationships to these groups and to the roles they demand, rather than focusing on any writer's roles. Susan, George, Doug, and Kris left the course not thinking of themselves as writers, but thinking of themselves as students, as people who would or would not succeed in college. Doug is the only student who explicitly conceived of a group of "writers" from his classroom experience, and he conceived of this group in order to disavow membership in it. When looked at from this perspective, these students thus learned very little about writing, for they were unable to connect the activities of writing to their sense of self in any significant way. For them, their experience in this writing classroom connected only to their roles as students and college people.

Looking at these students' identity negotiations, in short, allows us to highlight the limited nature of learning in this class. Although a number of powerful rhetorical strategies and principles were presented in the class, students left primarily aware of where they stood as students and college people. Any direct reflection on writing was secondary. By designing a course dominated by teacher-as-evaluator and teacher-as-diagnostician roles, I had functionally created a context where real learning about writing was unlikely to occur. The narrow context limited the roles available to students, and their learning was correspondingly narrow. If writing teachers really intend to help students develop important purposes, uses, and abilities for writing, then we need to present students with a different range of roles in our courses—and to accomplish this we need a different kind of classroom structure.

4 Writing, Reflection, and Intellectual Development: Teacher Change in a Piagetian-Based Class

If the course described in the last chapter is finally a call for change, the course described in this chapter is a description of how teachers come to make changes in their classrooms. The process of teacher change is extremely complicated. In my own practice as a teacher, for example, change has been a slow, gradual process. During the class described in chapter 3, I knew something was wrong, but I was not at all sure what this "something" was.

In the next few years, I experimented with different course organizations, trying to develop an alternative which might produce other results. Each change in organization was based in how I understood my teaching goals and options at the time, so the transformation of my classrooms paralleled my growing understanding of my purposes in teaching writing. Sometimes my understanding was further advanced than my practice, and sometimes my practice led my understanding. I tried several other sorts of classes (writing across the curriculum, writing for special purposes, and personal writing classes) before stumbling onto writing workshops as a possibility. In all of these attempts, I was guided by conversations with other teachers, by my reading and thinking, and by my continued experience with students—that is, by my own ongoing process of identity negotiation with the groups that made up my professional life.

The course described in this chapter is a powerful example of these complexities of teacher change. The teacher, Joy Ritchie, went through a similar process of identity negotiation as her course progressed. This negotiation involved her stance towards the kind of writing and learning she was promoting and her stance towards academic learning in general.

During the semester, Joy changed from accepting a focus on Piagetian intellectual development (as applied to writing) to a focus on writing as a means of reflecting and commenting on individual experience. As the course went on, she worked hard to decide for herself whether she accepted Piagetian intellectual development as the basis of her course. She worried about the model of "being a writer" that she presented and its relevance to the students' own lives and voices. Joy found herself engaged in ongoing critical thinking about her course (and her place in the university). This thinking led to slow changes in how her assignments progressed and to a completely new syllabus the following semester. These changes meant positioning herself in new ways relative to important groups in her department, profession, and community.

Because of this teacher's changing stances towards her roles, this course produced different tensions from the one described in chapter 3. Students initially thought their classroom experience was like the English classrooms they had been in before—they wrote papers on assigned topics, read literature and discussed it, and were supposed to learn something from these activities. The structure of the classroom thus put less strain on their identities as students than the audience course did, because the teacher-student relationships were more familiar.

As the class progressed, however, the teacher encouraged students to think about their roles, to explore their lives in relation to other lives, and to consider the place of writing in these processes. The class came to present a reflective attitude towards experience, tacitly asking students to take on a role which questioned their assumed stances towards their lives. In this way, the course came to model a different kind of role and encouraged students to try it out. Much of the ongoing tensions of the classroom involved student response to this modeled way of being a thinker-writer-explorer of experience.

In responding to the class, students therefore found themselves negotiating their relationships to these changing classroom roles. Some students found them extremely useful and molded them into a part of their developing identities. Others found only one of the two roles pertinent and engaged in selective compliance and rejection. Still others mixed the roles together, functionally combining parts of each and being confused by other parts. The ways they negotiated their own identities in relation to the modeled roles thus influenced how they understood their learning of writing.

I was fortunate to be a participant-observer in this course, which met during the spring of 1986 at the University of Nebraska.

The Course

The progress of this course exemplifies some of the complexity of changing one's approach to composition instruction. From an identity negotiations perspective, the process of change, for teachers as well as students, involves working out new roles for the self and new stances towards old roles. Change requires (1) perceiving some problem or inadequacy with an established role, (2) perceiving or constructing a new role for the self, and (3) altering one's relationship to the old role because of the new.

Because the process of change involves these shifting roles and relationships, it appears to be created by what Erving Goffman calls "underlife." Underlife is a normal feature of social interaction: whenever individuals are cast into a social role by a social organization (as teacher or student, as boss or employee), they are likely to exhibit behavior which shows there is more to them than that role suggests. Such behavior demonstrates that, even though they may fulfill their role obligations, people are far more complicated and hold other values and play other roles in other contexts. Thus, within any social interaction, role behavior and underlife behavior consistently occur. Underlife allows individuals a means of asserting their uniqueness while also complying with social demands.

Underlife in any social interaction occurs because individuals are always more complicated than any single role might imply. Individuals usually hold contradictory stances towards the behavior demanded by any given role. Goffman suggests that underlife is a normal means of relieving the tension of role performance and, as such, is usually "contained" within the social group, because its purpose is to provide a little breathing room for individuals within their role. Goffman distinguishes such "contained underlife" from "disruptive underlife," which seeks to alter the existing social roles and change the nature of interaction. Sometimes a little breathing room is not enough, and individuals realize that they must work towards a new way of interacting, towards a different set of roles for the self.

Although Goffman does not make this point, the route to change in a classroom (or any social setting) is clearly a progression from contained to disruptive underlife. As we take part in any of our roles, we notice little inconsistencies, little problems, in how those roles connect with our other activities. Normally, we just make a little joke like "I'd rather be fishing" and get on with the task at hand, but occasionally the little inconsistencies build up to a point where they cannot be ignored. We then find ourselves motivated to disrupt the existing pattern of interaction and to substitute a new one. This occasional process is the process of change.

In tracing Joy Ritchie's changes as a teacher during her 1986 spring semester course, I am describing exactly such a progression from contained to disruptive underlife. She began the course by operating out of an established role for her, the role of a University of Nebraska teacher guiding students through a Piagetian-based writing curriculum called ADAPT (Accent on Developing Advanced Processes of Thought).

She had some initial feelings of discomfort with this role, but they were not powerful enough for her to change her allegiance to the ADAPT program. As the course went on, however, her discomfort grew and her desire to try something new increased, until finally she found herself trying something entirely different with her class. For Joy, it was a progression from contained to disruptive underlife that led to change, and it is the possibility of such a progression that makes change in teaching generally possible.

Background: The Nebraska ADAPT Program

Joy's experience in the course I observed began in her prior teaching in the Nebraska ADAPT program, long before the course itself actually started. At the time I observed her class, Joy had taught as an adjunct visiting professor in the English department for two years. This position required her to teach a number of overload sections of first-year composition, to serve as administrative assistant for the Nebraska Writing Project, and to teach for the ADAPT program. As a nontenure track professor, she also felt pressured to publish, hoping to persuade the department to grant her tenure track status. In her position in the department, Joy was consequently pulled in several directions.

The course I observed was a regular overload section of first-year composition. Before the class started, Joy told me she intended to follow the ADAPT syllabus she had used the semester before with Bob Bergstrom, an ADAPT program developer. She had not been completely happy with that course, but thought it went well enough that she did not need to change the syllabus radically. Joy's course thus emerged from the Nebraska ADAPT program.

ADAPT is an interdisciplinary Piagetian-based program which aims to foster intellectual development during the first college year. In theory, the program's purpose is to help students move from Piaget's "concrete operational" to his "formal operational" stage of intellectual development. In the ADAPT handbook, *Multidisciplinary Piagetian-Based Programs for College Freshmen*, this move is described in the following terms:

> In the concrete stage the child could simultaneously put an object in multiple kinds of categories. Moving from these concrete kinds of labels, the child in the stage of formal thought can now reason about objects which cannot be seen or experienced concretely, such as the principle of inertia. The most dramatic change from concrete to formal operations is evidenced in a shift from focusing on the realities of the world to a consideration of the total possibilities that might exist in the world. In fact, once formal

operations are attained, the actualities of the world are secondary
in a person's thought processes to the range of possibilities which
might exist. For this reason, thought is more flexible. (2–3)

Drawing on survey data which suggests that up to 50 percent of first-
year college students are not yet functioning at the formal operational
level, the ADAPT staff consequently wanted to stimulate students'
intellectual development from concrete to formal operational thought.
This goal was justified because formal thought is "more flexible," more
"mature," and more characteristic of the kind of thought required in
academic study than concrete operational thought.

In practice, ADAPT courses in each discipline present students with
"learning cycles" which seek to move from concrete experience to
abstract thought and back to new applications to experience. The idea
of these learning cycles stems from Piaget's insistence that all learning
begins with sensorimotor experience. ADAPT teachers consequently
help students (1) explore an aspect of their experience through direct
observation and manipulation, (2) invent some kind of explanatory
principle for this experience, and (3) apply this principle to other
experiences. With repeated exposure to such a learning cycle, students
are encouraged to think more flexibly about experience and hence are
helped to move from concrete to formal operational thought.

In English classes, there is little direct manipulation of experience
in the way that, for example, a physics class can have students move
pendulums, take them apart, and put them together in different ways
in an effort to explore how they work. Similarly, there are no exact or
mathematical principles, comparable to the formulas of physics, for
describing experience. Writing and reading, as actions in the world,
are hence not as easily described by using Piaget's concrete and formal
operational categories. The English ADAPT staff, consequently, was
faced with the problem of adjusting ADAPT principles to English
classes. In dealing with this problem, staff members have continued to
evolve a variety of methods.

At the time of this study, the English ADAPT teachers resolved the
problem by adopting Young, Becker, and Pike's *Rhetoric: Discovery
and Change*, which presented a set of heuristics for thinking about
communication. (Since this study was conducted—and as a consequence of Joy Ritchie's continued input to the program—the English
ADAPT program has significantly changed, now no longer emphasizing
this text.) Young, Becker, and Pike's heuristics depend on "formal
operational" thought, though they are aimed at the understanding and
practice of writing. In the fall of 1986, the teachers argued that if
students became able to understand and use these heuristics, they

would be well on their way to formal operational thought (at least about the subject of communication).

In 1986, English ADAPT courses were consequently structured around the various heuristics of Young, Becker, and Pike's text. In the opinion of these teachers, two of these heuristics are most important for writing. The first is Maxim 4, which states that anything a person can think about can be described as a static object, an object changing in time and space, and an object operating within a network of relations to other objects. The second is Maxim 5, which states that humans can communicate only if they share enough information so that new information from one party can be easily understood by the other.

In English ADAPT courses, the learning cycles of the classroom are designed primarily around these two maxims. Most learning cycles follow a set pattern: (1) students are helped to explore some aspect of their experience through guided classroom exercises (exploration); (2) they then write a paper from this exploration and discuss the paper with other members of the class (invention); (3) they are then asked to change their approach to the paper in some describable way, thus applying what they have invented to another aspect of their experience (application).

To introduce the idea of shifting perspective on experience, for example, many ADAPT English courses begin with a "favorite place" assignment. First, students in class are asked to draw maps of a favorite place they remember. While they draw, the teacher leads them through a guided exploration exercise by asking questions about different aspects of this place which they may or may not want to include on their maps. The students are given time to talk about the maps with each other. Second, students write a paper about this favorite place. The activity of writing means that they must make some choices about how to present their place, and some of the material from their exploration is left out. Students then share these drafts with others in small groups. Lastly, students are asked to write another paper which changes the perspective or focus on the place. For example, one student in the class I studied wrote his second paper from the point of view of an apple hanging on a tree in his backyard, instead of describing this backyard from his own point of view. Such a sequence of assignments follows the idea of the learning cycle carefully.

As in the audience-based course presented in chapter 3, the guiding idea of these ADAPT courses is an improvement in thinking more than in writing, a development of thought rather than a development of any particular text or writing skill. The teacher-student relationship that ADAPT courses intended to establish in 1986 is a version of the diagnostician-to-developing-adolescent relationship discussed in the last chapter. The teacher holds information about thinking processes which the student does not have and evaluates the students' overall progression in attaining these thinking processes through a series of structured exercises.

Course Design and Teacher Rationale

The course Joy Ritchie taught during spring semester 1986 began with her experience teaching in the ADAPT program. In the preceding semester, she and Bob Bergstrom had team-taught an ADAPT English course, but she had not been assigned an ADAPT course for the spring. Instead, she had been given three sections of Composition 118, a first-year writing and reading course. This assignment, in conjunction with her other duties—helping to administer the Nebraska Writing Project and acting as participant-observer in another English department classroom—constituted an overload in the department's employment scheme. Partly because of her work overload, Joy told me before the class began that she intended to "do" Bob's ADAPT course in her 118 sections because it would save time, although she had mixed feelings about that course. Her mixed feeling came from a sense that her various duties (especially her work with ADAPT and the Nebraska Writing Project) offered her conflicting ideas about how to teach writing.

As the course progressed, Joy's mixed feelings about ADAPT theory and practice led to more and more revision in her approach to her own course. Instead of a course aimed at the development of formal operational thought, Joy's course slowly transformed into a course which modeled a certain way of being a writer. Instead of the ADAPT sequence of papers all leading to an understanding of heuristics for communication, Joy began to loosen her assignments, to allow students greater freedom in the directions they took, and to focus on using writing as a means of exploring thoughts and communicating with readers.

In short, as the course progressed, its purpose changed. Where it began with a developmental purpose (students would improve their level of thinking by working through a series of exercises), it ended with a modeling purpose (students were presented a model of how writers behave and were encouraged to try out these behaviors themselves). In the semester that followed this course, Joy abandoned the ADAPT format entirely for a workshop teaching format, because it allowed her to model more effectively how writers act, think, and relate to experience.

The course proved to be very successful, as measured by student evaluations at the end of the semester—most students gave both teacher and course the highest possible marks. Because her mixed feelings about the course design were present from the beginning, her changes in the class did not seem like radical shifts, but instead were perceived as a gradual development of trends that had been operating all along. In the section that follows, I will describe the course as it began and as it changed, emphasizing the instructor's changing stance towards her own teaching.

Beginnings

When I interviewed Joy the week before spring semester classes began, she already spoke of several problems with her proposed course. She began by saying that she intended to teach "the same course" she and Bob Bergstrom had taught the semester before, a course structured around six two-week learning cycles. She had particularly liked using Margaret Laurence's *A Bird in the House* in the ADAPT context. Joy did, however, have three reservations about that course. First, she felt somewhat uncomfortable with its "tight structure" (an idea she did not elaborate on). Second, she had reservations about using *Rhetoric: Discovery and Change* as her primary text. She felt that last semester's class was "trying to hammer it home rather than setting it before the students and engaging them and letting go" and that there was a sort of unacknowledged "undercurrent of how writers develop" operating in her previous use of the text which she wished could be brought more into focus. Third, she expressed worries about the "teacher center-stage role" in ADAPT classes—a role she admitted liking because of the "limelight" it offered, but a role she worried about because, as she said, the "dramatic, commanding role of ADAPT professors—how manipulative is it?"

At this point, she was not overly worried about these ambivalences. She just noted them as "reservations" she had going into the class. She began the course, in other words, expressing contained underlife— some reservations concerning the role she was about to play which showed that she did not merely embrace that role; not enough reservations to cause her to disrupt the social interaction of the ADAPT class itself.

For the first four weeks of spring semester, Joy followed the previous semester's course fairly rigidly. Her syllabus established the same system of grading, and her assignments proceeded as they had before. Grades, she explained, would be assigned on a contract system:

> For any grade above a "D," all the basic requirements of the course must be met. You must attend regularly, participate faithfully in your group, submit daily informal journals on time, do the reading, and write the drafts and the final copies of papers [six pairs in all]. A failure to do any of these things will result in a lower grade, whatever your performance may be.
>
> For a "C"—all the requirements plus *two* papers accepted.
>
> For a "B"—all the requirements plus *four* papers accepted.
>
> For an "A"—all the requirements plus *six* papers accepted, two of which must be of high quality. ("Grading" section from instructor's syllabus)

Students were required to meet basic expectations and then could work for the grade of their choice by negotiating teacher "acceptance" of some of their papers. In class, she explained that her idea of "acceptance" might seem kind of vague, but that with each student she would negotiate until both student and teacher felt the paper was ready to be accepted. Acceptance was thus a kind of quality judgment about the paper, but not a judgment as fixed as a letter grade. This contract system for assigning grades had been used in her fall semester ADAPT course (and variants of it are used in most English department ADAPT courses) because it allows some student control over the grades they will be assigned, leaving the teacher free to work for cognitive development without having to grade for it.

The first two learning cycles and the accompanying pairs of papers also replicated what she and Bob had done the previous semester:

Papers 1 and 2: Students explored through map-drawing and readings some favorite places they (and others) remembered. Then they wrote a description of a place they remembered from their childhood that was important to them. The second paper involved changing the focus on the scene they described.

Papers 3 and 4: Students explored through guided discussion and readings some experiences from which they (and others) had learned. Then students wrote about such an experience, the purpose being to help the reader share both the experience and what it taught them. For the second paper in this set, students were asked to think about how they went about changing some important idea they had held about the world, focusing this time on the process of change that led to their present understanding of the situation.

Classroom activities during this period supported the learning cycles and derived from what she and Bob had done the previous semester. In general, Mondays were spent either exploring a new paper topic or reading papers aloud in small groups; Wednesdays were spent discussing readings from *The Bedford Reader* (Kennedy and Kennedy) or *A Bird in the House;* and Fridays were spent working through ideas from *Rhetoric: Discovery and Change.* On this format, Mondays were explicitly a writing day, Wednesdays were used to explore how someone else had thought about the sort of topic students were working on, and Fridays were used as "thinking about thinking" days (where students would step back from the direct experiences of Monday and Wednesday and reflect on general principles at work in their understanding of experience).

During the first four weeks, both Joy and I noticed radical differences in how students responded to these activities. Mondays and Wednesdays invariably went well—students enjoyed exploration activities and reading aloud to each other on Mondays and were generally fascinated on the Wednesdays that *A Bird in the House* was discussed. Fridays, however, were another matter. As soon as Young, Becker, and Pike was opened, students became quiet, stopped volunteering comments, and raised questions about Monday's assignment or standards for acceptable papers rather than addressing the ideas in the text.

In terms of the developmental purpose of the class, this pattern of response was a problem. The "thinking about thinking" material from Young, Becker, and Pike was in many ways at the heart of the progression that students were supposed to make from concrete to formal operational thinking. Yet it was this material that they resisted. They enjoyed the other course activities more than these formal thinking activities. In interviews, Joy said that this pattern of student response was "a constant feature" of ADAPT English classes, but that, with two professors in the room, "pushing Young, Becker, and Pike is easier."

Transitions

At the end of the first four weeks, Joy explicitly made what she felt was a transition in the course. She felt motivated to make this change because of the pattern of student response described above and what was happening in students' writing. During an interview before the fifth week began, Joy explained her intended transition. She thought she saw "people having some things on their own agenda to work with—a more open-ended assignment would allow them to go their own directions a bit more."

"That *ain't* ADAPT way," she said humorously, "but it's where I'm at right now."

Joy felt that the next learning cycle's pair of papers on the syllabus had not worked well the previous semester (students were assigned to write a description of a person they knew well, and then a description of how that person viewed them—last time, they "hated the second description"). Hence she was willing to make a change. She also felt like "part of the script was missing" for her class, because she had no other teacher in the classroom with her. She still felt committed to the ADAPT model, but also sensed that something was not working in her class and that she needed to make a change. She seemed undecided about how the class was going and unsure whether the problems were a consequence of the ADAPT syllabus and purpose or whether these problems should be blamed on her own inadequacies as a teacher.

She made her ambivalence about the course clear when I asked her what she hoped her students would articulate for themselves as a consequence of taking her class:

> To find they are very interesting people, and have rich experience (which they may write about) and to see also how that's connected with a whole community of experiences that they're a part of—their experience connects with Laurence, with experiences in reading—a sense that "I am not alone in the world—I am unique with a set of unique experiences, but I'm not so unique that I'm not part of a community of people with similar experiences."
>
> Other connections: to think about and monitor—and I'll push them—I want them to become more aware of how they think and solve problems, how we operate in groups to solve problems, and some ways of looking at and working with things they don't understand. (Interview notes, February 1986)

In stating what she hoped students would articulate, Joy presented two distinct purposes. The first purpose she mentioned is not directly a developmental purpose. Instead, it involves students "seeing themselves" in a certain way. At this point in the class, Joy described this way of seeing themselves as recognizing both that they are unique, interesting persons and that they belong to a community of writers and readers which values such uniqueness. In articulating this purpose for her class, she was thus beginning to think about students' experience of self, about student identity, as it connects with a community of writers.

Joy's second purpose was more developmental and more closely aligned with the ADAPT program. It involved "becoming more aware of how they think"; it involved thinking about thinking. She committed herself to this purpose ("I'll push them"), but presented it second when she thought about her course.

At the five-week point, then, Joy was aware of two contradictory directions she wanted her course to go. One direction was that provided by the ADAPT program. She felt responsible to this program and its directions, and seemed to blame herself for the ways in which her course was not living up to ADAPT purposes. The other direction involved helping students experience themselves as writers, understood as experiencing both their uniqueness and their membership in a group of writers who are interested in reflecting on experience. Still trying to maintain her connection to ADAPT, Joy had taken a step towards disruptive underlife, towards recasting the roles of her classroom. At this point in the semester, her goal was more a revision of the ADAPT class than a substitution of a new format.

In the weeks that followed, however, Joy slowly came to accept that her purpose was helping students experience themselves as writers, and that this purpose was finally different from ADAPT's purpose. Her sequence of assignments became, in her words, progressively "looser" so that students would have more opportunity for exploring their own purposes and topics in writing. Her stance towards the course, as weekly interview notes show, became increasingly more comfortable with this new direction.

Where papers one through four in the first two learning cycles had explicitly followed the old syllabus, papers five through twelve, the last four pairs of papers which would have made up the remaining four learning cycles, grew more and more connected to students' own experience as writers.

Papers 5 and 6: Students wrote about a "phase" someone they knew had gone through, describing for their readers what had happened and how they understood it. For their revision, students were encouraged to expand their description by considering interviews with this person or others who knew him or her, other people's views on this phase, and any long-term changes in which the phase played a part. These revisions were suggested under the general rubric of "making the paper more appropriate for a wider audience."

Papers 7 and 8: Students were given a choice to write about: their own futures as they imagined them, our collective future in the country or world, or the values and influences that got them to where they are now. Joy met with each student individually to negotiate revisions for each paper instead of assigning a universal second paper.

Papers 9 and 10: Students were asked to write about a problem they had with someone they knew or an issue they felt strongly about. They were to write the piece to the other people involved. For revision, Joy brought in some student papers (and some of her own letters) as examples, and focused on audience response—what attitudes, assumptions, beliefs might shape their reactions, and how a writer might choose to come across to get them to listen. Students were encouraged to revise with these points in mind.

Papers 11 and 12: Students were told they could write on anything they wanted, and revisions were individually negotiated. Joy suggested a range of ideas, from taking stock of their first college year to extending ideas from their informal journals or other papers, to reflecting on their fourteen-plus years of school.

As the course progressed, Joy basically abandoned the learning cycle structure of pairs of papers and instead had students revise their first papers in light of the small group discussions and their conferences with her. She continued to suggest topics which invited students to explore their own experience, but began focusing more and more on having their description of this experience connect with their readers. She ended the course with an open set of papers in which students could choose their own topic.

Each of these changes supported the emergent purpose for her course—modeling how writers reflect on experience and helping students reflect and write this way themselves. Most of these changes pulled away from the explicit learning cycle of the ADAPT program and its focus on the communication maxims of Young, Becker, and Pike. Her course thus evolved towards one that modeled how reflective writers behave and away from the ADAPT "intellectual development" course she began with.

These changes in assignments were paralleled by changes in Joy's stance towards her purpose and ADAPT's purpose. She slowly came to support and feel comfortable with her "modeling" purpose and to accept that her "inability" as a teacher was not the reason she felt stress with the ADAPT syllabus. In weeks six through eight, she described herself by using images of ambivalence—the "Ambivalent Writing Teacher," the inexperienced horse team driver, the tightrope—as weekly interview notes show:

> 2/20/86 (6th week): Joy suggests I write about this class using the title "The Ambivalent Writing Teacher." She feels excited that "papers are becoming more genuine, about subjects they really wanted to write about and were important to them," but also feels "tension about her role of teacher manipulating her" because many of the students may be only writing stuff that *looks* like they really care about it in order to please her.

> 2/27/86 (7th week): Joy is thinking about "departing more from the syllabus," she feels "odd about re-using Bob's syllabus, almost trapped by it, getting less and less comfortable as time goes on." She's thinking about changing abruptly now, recognizing she's "behind" on the old syllabus "because of more in-class writing and group work." She wants to ask me next week about changes she's thought of, and talks explicitly about how there's a tradition

in participant-observation work of intervention or suggested change on the teacher's part as a consequence of what's observed.

3/6/86 (8th week): Joy describes herself as shifting daily in her class—she uses the image of a driver of a team of horses, how an experienced driver keeps all the reins going to control the team and keep the wagon on the road. She feels like her wagon will stay on the road, but there's a lot of play in it, as if she's an inexperienced driver. Says she enjoys being on the tightrope, trying to keep the reins going.

In week nine, however, she expressed a need to "redo" her course by changing the ADAPT program emphasis away from Young, Becker, and Pike to Margaret Laurence. At this point, she had become less ambivalent and had decided that what she was now trying to accomplish was more important than what the ADAPT program had been doing:

3/13/86 (9th week): Joy talks about how to "redo" her course, making two suggestions. First, she would improve the course by using Young Becker and Pike "covertly" if at all. Second, she would focus more on Margaret Laurence's book. In class, she has abandoned explicit discussion of Young Becker and Pike and instead is using Fridays to discuss more reading, do more small group work, and explore topics more.

From that point on, she talked about her course in a new way—in terms of "why we write," in terms of the importance of reflecting on experience, in terms of differences she felt between her own experience as a writer and her students' experiences as writers:

4/5/86 (12th week): I write out an ordered list of what Joy's "goals" for the course seem to be (from observation)—a list she confirms in interview: (1) She wants students to see themselves as interesting people with a lot to offer, to recognize that their lives and experiences are interesting and worthwhile. (2) She wants students to see that there's a lot they don't know about themselves and their experiences, that it's okay not to know, and that it's important to try to investigate experience to be able to know oneself/one's world better. (3) She wants students to see writing as a way of investigating, thinking about, understanding experience—consequently, most assignments are focused on using writing to explore one's thought and experience—consequently, she focuses on what can be understood about people in *Bird in the House*. (4) She wants students to understand something of how to succeed in writing to an audience—besides "writing to explore," she sees "writing to do, to change readers' minds."

The goals of her class had thus shifted from trying to help students develop intellectually to trying to help them understand and act as writers, to help them see themselves as part of a larger community of writers and readers who are interested in reflecting on experience:

> 4/17/86 (13th week): I make the comment that as the course is winding up Joy seems to be "hammering home" connections between writing, reading, and literature. In response, Joy says she feels *Bird in the House* to be a great book, really useful in presenting "what we all have to face," very explanatory. She started a letter to Margaret Laurence and expects to write an article on teaching this book to first year students after a while— feels a problem of really feeling this to be powerful and important in her life, and not having it connect as strongly with theirs. Really wants to make explicit at least the questions "why do we write? why do we read? what do we gain from reading other writers' work and other students' work?" in the time remaining. Is worried that her new Friday activities (visiting the student art gallery, interviewing as a class a student artist) won't connect.

As Joy progressed through her course, she became confident in her own goals and very concerned with the effectiveness of her teaching in relation to these goals. Her emergent goals focused on reflective writing and were, in her mind, modeled by Margaret Laurence. She came to see herself as promoting a model of how writers reflect on experience and as providing a classroom environment where students could "try on" this modeled way of reflecting. Her course became an attempt to model and support an "identity" of sorts for writers, an identity which was very much based on the stance towards experience which Laurence took in *A Bird in the House*. It was a stance based on reflection about the roles one plays and the purposes for those roles, on communicating what one learns in reflection, and on considering the kind of community one communicates within.

In coming to these conclusions as a teacher, Joy shifted in her allegiances to her department's groups and in the roles she made available for her students. She had moved through contained underlife to disruptive underlife, from an initial point where she wanted only a little breathing room for herself within the old ADAPT role to a final point where it was necessary to create new roles for herself as teacher and to reject most of the old ADAPT roles.

Classroom Roles for Students and Writers

Joy's course presented students with two distinct roles in the classroom: a student role defined by the developmental ADAPT program, and a writer role defined through the example of Margaret Laurence. Each of these roles suggested a different teacher-student relationship.

1. *The student role:* teacher as diagnostician; student as developing adolescent. In keeping with the developmental purpose of the ADAPT program, the teacher was set up as someone more interested in students' overall changes in development than in their success or failure on any specific class task. Consequently, students did not receive grades on their work. Instead papers, when returned from the teacher, had comments on them which usually encouraged students to think about other aspects of their topic. By having final grades depend on negotiating "acceptance" of pairs of papers from each learning cycle instead of on the accumulation of points or average grades on individual papers, the teacher-student relationship was directly focused on the kinds of thinking demonstrated by each pair of papers.

Furthermore, in the initial weeks of class, the focus on Young, Becker, and Pike's textbook, with its emphasis on general formal possibilities for thinking, supported the diagnostician-to-developing-adolescent relationship. By directly naming and exposing general maxims for thought, the course drew attention to processes for thinking that the teacher used and students might or might not yet use. This aspect of the teacher-student relationship was further highlighted by the use of reading material from *The Bedford Reader*, which at least initially served as a place where general patterns of thinking and communication could be identified.

2. *The writer role:* writers as reflectors on experience and communicators of reflection. As the course progressed, Joy led students from focusing only on general traits of thinking and communication to considering their families, pasts, and events and why someone might write about such things. She used writing-reading-thinking-talking to explore social life and to communicate ideas about what had been explored. In both of these activities, Laurence's *A Bird in the House* served as a model, first of what might be thought about, later of how a writer might behave. In Joy's hands, *A Bird in the House* came to offer two kinds of opportunities for students: an opportunity to think about lives in the way Joy had them think about the book, and an opportunity to act as writers like Laurence, using writing to explore the complexity of their own lives and to communicate this complexity to other readers.

One of the tensions in *A Bird in the House* is the tension between the fanciful, escapist stories people would like to tell themselves and the real, difficult stories that people live. The book, in fact, chronicles the development of the young Vanessa through a childhood in which she writes escapist plots about pirates and explorers to a realization of the intense honesty required to write from real life.

Although not explicitly stated in the novel, this same Vanessa grows in time to write *A Bird in the House*, a book which scrupulously details events from this character's childhood. Writing, for Vanessa, comes to be a tool for honest exploration of her own life instead of a tool for escape. The difficulty of real life and of understanding it thus becomes one of the central aspects of the novel, and writing for Vanessa becomes one of the ways of exploring these difficulties. One deals in writing with the troubling complexity of even the most mundane lives, as she learns when she hears about a letter her father, Ewen, wrote to tell his mother of the wartime death of his brother:

> "Ewen never spoke of it to me," my mother went on, "until once his mother showed me the letter he'd written her at the time. It was a peculiar letter, almost formal, saying how gallantly Rod had died, and all that. I guess I shouldn't have, but I told him she'd shown it to me. He was very angry that she had. And then, as though for some reason he were terribly ashamed, he said—*I had to write something to her, but men don't really die like that, Beth. It wasn't that way at all.*" (48; Laurence's italics)

The problem of what to tell, how to understand it to tell it, and the courage required to be honest enough to tell it all come together as central ingredients in the process of writing.

The role of the writer in Laurence's novel is of a person who uses writing to explore, present, and hopefully understand the complexity of life around her. This role, furthermore, is presented as difficult because of the intense honesty it requires of the self, and the recognition of the tendency to escape from this honesty into self-protecting fantasy. The writer is a kind of intrepid explorer of the self, requiring as much stamina and bravery as exploring any other unknown regions.

It was this sense of writer as explorer that Joy's course came to model. Joy used Laurence's book to model a certain stance towards experience, a certain way of writing and thinking in response to experience. More and more as the course progressed, she pointed explicitly to Laurence (and implicitly to herself) as a model of the sort of person who typically approaches the world this way, and suggested that writing allows and depends on exactly such an approach. Her emergent goal, then, was to improve students' writing and reading by encouraging them to see themselves as language-users like Laurence, using writing to explore the complexity of experience and to communicate what they find.

The way Joy connected this book to the structure of her course and the way she handled class discussion contributed to the presentation of this role as a valid model of how to be a writer. Her assignments all asked students to explore some aspect of their experience and thought. As the course developed, these assignments also asked students to share what they found with their readers. Furthermore, Joy drew connections between Laurence's writing and the students' assignments. When students wrote about an experience from which they learned, they read about the birth of Vanessa's brother and Grandmother MacLeod's demand that he be named after the dead Rodrick. As they wrote about a phase, they read about Grandmother Connor's death and the "mask" that Grandfather put on. And so on.

Later in the course, when students were writing to an audience about issues and problems which concerned them, Joy brought Laurence's approach to writing explicitly into the picture. While discussing the last two chapters, she began to ask if ideas or patterns from these chapters connected with earlier chapters, and what Laurence might have been up to in writing this book. At the same time, she was asking students to come to grips in their own writing with real problems they faced and real readers who might think differently than they. On other days during this time, Joy brought in drafts of her own letters on such topics as her anger at sensationalist television newscasts and discussed how she had to work through her anger before she could write a persuasive letter. She took students to the student art gallery and asked one of the student artists to talk about why he painted what he painted. And in class she said things like "Is this story Margaret Laurence's essay #9?"

Through Laurence's writing, her own writing, and an analogy with artists' work, Joy's course presented students with a second role they could take on in the classroom: a role of a writer who reflects on experience and then seeks to communicate that reflection. This role was different from the ADAPT student role and cast the teacher-student relationship in a new light. While Joy as teacher still graded student work and progress according to the contract system established by the ADAPT syllabus, Joy as writer played another role, modeling the idea that students could be writers with their own subjects to explore and communicate, not just developing adolescents who needed to demonstrate to a diagnostician teacher a major change in thinking processes.

Student Response

In reacting to Joy's class, students needed to negotiate their own stances towards the particular student and writer roles her classroom made possible. The ways individual students came to position themselves towards these roles determined how they understood the course and their learning within it.

While the teacher's behavior presented students with two different roles they might respond to, these roles were not experienced as directly conflicting or contradictory. Unlike the course described in chapter 3, this course did not lead to student frustration and anger towards their experience. Instead, the very high student ratings of the class and teacher point to much greater comfort with classroom roles than in the audience-based class.

But student comfort with their experience does not directly show the kind of learning they engaged in during class. What students learned, as in the last class described, was also a product of the particular identity negotiations they became involved in.

As the course progressed, I followed eight students closely, conducting out-of-class interviews with them at three points during the semester. Of the eight students, two embraced the writer role and left the course excited about being writers, defending their excitement with explanations of writing and reading which were similar to those Joy had offered. Five other students felt good about the course and about their writing, but felt tense, confused, or uncertain about aspects of the roles Joy presented. These students all provided a rationale for their own sense of writing and themselves which justified their mixed reactions, often highlighting their role as developing student as more important than the role of reflective writer. The final student claimed to like Joy as a person, but rejected the course as a waste of time because it did not help her with what she thought writing was. This student in many ways fixated on a traditional good student role that never really operated in Joy's classroom, and her rejection of the course stemmed from her inability to make the course's roles fit the school context she imagined. In the section that follows, I will briefly describe four of these students' responses, using excerpts from my interviews with them to illuminate these general patterns.

Pattern One: Embracing the Writer Role

One of the students, Amy, exemplified most clearly an embracing of the modeled writer's role. In interviews, she articulated a connection between her writing and Laurence's and claimed that this connection contributed to writing in general. Furthermore, she connected these ideas to her sense of herself as a person outside the classroom.

According to Amy, the way she responded to *Bird in the House* and to the course in general was a function of the person she was. She described herself as someone who had always liked English courses, particularly courses with literature. For her, what was important about reading literature was what it allowed her to see about herself. This stance informed her positive evaluation of *Bird in the House:*

> I'm a people person I suppose that's why I like it. It's interesting to read about somebody else ... you can tie your family to things that happened in their family, you know, there's always somebody in your family that's either like Grandfather or Vanessa. (Final interview, spring 1986)

For Amy, the book was not really different from other books she had read in English class—the connection between reading and understanding one's own family was one she had already made. She thus understood the class's student role in a way familiar and comfortable to her. In English class, she expected to read material she liked and expected to think about and discuss this material in interesting ways. Her experience as student in Joy's class seemed very much like experiences she had had in her high school English classes.

When she turned to writing, however, Amy made much greater claims for this particular course. Although she had been presented before with the idea of reading as a way of exploring her own experience, she said she never had experienced writing this way. In her words, her past writing courses had forced her to copy forms; this course allowed her to use writing to explore and communicate:

> I think I've learned more in sixteen weeks here, how to write, than I have in like my three years of writing in high school. Here you had to write about what, your experience, what you wanted to write about and they told you what, you know, an audience to put it towards. I mean, in high school you were just writing because they wanted you to write something—you had to, you were, you practiced more on writing the, you know, correct form instead of how you felt about what you were writing and who your audience was for. (Final interview, spring 1986)

In Amy's mind, then, the course allowed her to connect reading and writing as activities in a new way. Following Joy's lead, she could now see writing as a way to explore experience, just as reading had been for her in the past. Her own writing, she could see, did not have to be overwhelmingly centered on "form" as it had been. Instead, it could be just like Laurence's writing—an exploration of experience. This new possibility created a new role for Amy as writer. Where in the past she had written only to fulfill a teacher's assignments (the narrow version of writing as test-taking we saw operating in the audience-based class of chapter 3), in this class she could try out a different role as writer. She could follow Laurence's example and use writing as a form of reflection and communication, a focus on "your experience, what you wanted to write about" and on "an audience to put it towards."

For Amy, the exciting part of the course was the idea that writing could be used to explore, understand, and communicate experience. She already saw herself as a person who was interested in understanding experience and who used reading for this purpose; writing thus became an added tool. Her acceptance of the role of writer as "one who explores experience" seemed primarily an embellishment of a stance she already held toward the world. Through Joy's course, she was able to connect the idea of writing to the sense of herself as a person she had already developed. The course with its stance towards writing and its support of an "understanding" stance towards people thus helped Amy further develop the sort of person she felt she already was.

Pattern Two: Role Combination and Clarification

While Amy articulated the connections between writing, reading, and experience that Joy came to model and felt good about seeing herself in this way, the most common response from a second group of students was to enjoy the experience, but to feel some nagging worries about it. Where Amy felt confirmed in the sort of person she was, several students felt both excited and threatened. In responding to the course, these students had to find a way of justifying their responses to themselves, of transforming their understanding of Joy's course so that they could keep what excited them and avoid what was threatening. I will describe the responses of two such students, Clark and Melody.

Clark

Clark's response to the course was twofold. On the one hand, he enjoyed the course. He particularly enjoyed the last, open assignment, during which he wrote a lengthy sword and sorcery story and revised the ending extensively (an experience he described as really fun and something he would remember in the years to come). He also pointed to two important things he had learned in class: the importance of audience, which was a concept he felt would help him in the future when he needed to speak in front of groups of people; and how to analyze "stuff" better, by which he meant how to read more critically. On the other hand, he disliked Laurence's book:

> *Clark:* Nothing ever, I mean nothing good ever happens in that book, it's always drab and morbid, I mean people are dying,

people are running away, people are going crazy.... The only good thing that happens is Aunt Edna gets married. The rest of it, I mean something good will start to happen and it turns bad.... I don't understand, she must [pause] had a bad life, she wrote, she wrote it from her own experience, 'cause, I mean, I've never known anybody that had that bad a life.... I mean, I hope my life never turns out like that.

Interviewer: So for you it was real depressing. Why do you think Joy chose to use it?

Clark: I don't know. [pause] I'd like to know. (Final interview, spring 1986)

Clark seemed uncertain about the experience Laurence's book presented. He found it puzzling and depressing, something he did not understand. The fact that so many hurtful things happened to the characters made him uncomfortable, especially when he reflected on his own life in comparison with theirs. He had his life planned out. For his seventh paper, Clark had written about his future, how after college he would become a fighter pilot in the Air Force, maybe get married, and have a successful career. He revised this paper to detail the steps he would go through to become a fighter pilot, rather than responding to any of Joy's queries about how he would feel if these goals did not come true or if he were not satisfied with them. In light of his own planned life, the twists of fate in Laurence's book were disturbing, and he hoped his life never turned out like that.

Rather than connect the experiences of reading and writing as Amy had (and begin reflecting on the potentially troubling events we all might face), Clark found he did not understand Laurence's book and resisted thinking about it. The consequence of his reaction, in terms of the roles Joy's course offered, was that Clark formed a useful student role for himself, but ignored or left untouched the kind of writer role that operated in the class.

By focusing on enjoying his sorcery paper and its revisions, learning about audience, and learning about analyzing reading, Clark kept his relationship to the course well within the ADAPT role of student as someone developing better processes of thought. He pointed to his work in the class, named the concepts he learned and the work he did to demonstrate this learning, and felt good about that experience. He saw himself, to put it briefly, as someone who had been a good student according to the available role. He had developed new ways of thinking and had demonstrated them in his revisions.

At the same time, he ignored more or less completely the particular role of reflective, communicative writer that Joy presented. He rejected the model of writing that Laurence presented as too depressing. He applied the concept of audience he so liked to speaking before groups of people rather than to writing (in fact, he said he doubted he would do much writing as a fighter pilot). And the analysis he learned applied to reading, not to writing.

Clark responded to the class by segmenting his experience of it into discrete parts. When I asked him explicitly if he saw connections between the reading and the writing, he said he could not see any. When I asked him to summarize what he might remember about the course in the future, he responded with a list of disconnected things— he had learned how important audience is, he had learned how to analyze stuff, and he expected he would keep his last paper because he liked it. Instead of perceiving the activities of the class as a whole, Clark separated them and, in separating them, obscured the writer role Joy modeled. This separation allowed him to justify his differing responses to the parts of the course—he could remain puzzled and scornful of Laurence's book, but he could also hold on to his positive sense of his own writing, his positive sense of Joy, and the idea of the importance of audience for speaking.

What emerges from Clark's response, then, is a division of Joy's course into two roles, which can be responded to separately. On one side is Laurence's book and the whole way of exploring experience which it represents. On the other is the idea of thinking strategies he could adopt in order to succeed better in the future. Clark kept the two separate and consequently could see the first as worthless or unintelligible ("Do authors really put all that stuff in there?"), the second as useful. Such a division allowed him to protect his sense of self while still admitting he liked the course—he could keep the elements of the course that proved useful to his "planned" life and eliminate the elements that challenged it.

Melody

Unlike Clark, Melody entered the course seeing herself as a writer. As a theater arts major, she described herself as associated with creative writers and actors and really interested in writing. During the semester, she confirmed this sense of herself by joining an experimental theater group and writing for and acting in four improvisational one-act plays. Nevertheless, Melody's response to the course was similar to Clark's. She combined the roles of student and writer being offered by the course in a way which preserved her current sense of herself and consequently understood her experience with Laurence's book as an unimportant part of the course.

A lengthy passage from my final interview with Melody illuminates these transformations:

> *Interviewer:* In these last two weeks, we haven't done much actual writing, instead we've finished *Bird in the House* and gone to the art gallery. Why do you think we're doing it?
>
> *Melody:* I don't know, I think it still has to do with writing though, 'cause when we went over to the gallery we were writing about what we were looking at. It makes you look more as to not just what you're writing but why you're writing it and what makes you write it. 'Cause every week we get deeper into it, deeper into why we're writing, you know, than what we're writing. Instead of just the basic rules of writing. . . .
>
> *Interviewer:* This *Bird in the House* is the only book we've read all of. What are we supposed to get out of this?
>
> *Melody:* I don't know.
>
> *Interviewer:* Do you think it connects with the writing?
>
> *Melody:* Yes, some of it does. But, as many people have said the book is so morbid in itself that you really don't think about what it's teaching you or what you're learning from it, you just think how morbid it is. . . . I figured we read it because she's a good writer, a good way of writing. . . . I just figured she wrote it because she wanted to write it, it was semi-autobiographical and you know, why else would you write, you know. I don't really see a purpose for writing all this. (Final interview, spring 1986)

Melody showed on the one hand an insightful awareness that Joy's course had slowly been moving towards the question "why do we write?"—a question Melody found exciting. She had a sense of an answer: We write, she seemed to say, to communicate and explore thoughts. She saw the exploration of "what makes us write" as exciting, and saw many aspects of the course converging at this point. Like Amy, she also saw this focus on "why we write" as an exciting contrast with her earlier classes, which had focused instead on "rules of writing." The image of writer which Melody seemed to be developing was an image of someone driven to write, perhaps by parts of her personal history, and of someone who writes to communicate with others. Much of the writer role which Joy modeled is encapsulated in such an image.

But Melody finally did not connect this answer with *Bird in the House*. She claimed that the book probably did connect, but that she found it so morbid she stopped thinking about it. For her, the particular stance Laurence provides was not important to her sense of writers as people who explore and communicate—she could accept being a writer without accepting the depressing events of Laurence's book. As she explained, she did not like to think about morbid things.

This rationale seemed connected to her sense of herself as a theater person. Melody came from a wealthy Omaha family and was excited about her future as an actress and playwright, but frightened that she would not succeed (fears she wrote about in her seventh and eighth papers). The thought of life not turning out positively, but closing in as it did for the MacLeods and Connors, may have been more than she could accept at this point in her life. In this way, Melody was very much like Clark—both responded to their experience in Joy's class in ways which eliminated those roles that threatened their sense of self, but both also kept a version of those roles which supported that sense of self.

In Melody's case, however, much of the writer role Joy presented was incorporated into the roles she accepted. Where Clark could keep only the ADAPT student role of someone improving his thinking processes (functionally rejecting anything that had directly to do with writing), Melody's model of the writer kept the idea of self-exploration and the idea of communication with readers, leaving out only the possibility that the self to be explored is a self in a depressing environment. What Melody learned in class was more complex than what Clark learned. She learned much about "why we write," and the thinking processes that she adopted as a good student in Joy's class are processes directly related to writing. Like Amy, Melody combined the student and writer roles of the course in a way that was useful to her growing sense of herself as a writer; like Clark, she did not think about the depressing elements of Laurence's book.

Pattern Three: Rejection

Not all students saw connections between the course and their own writing, however. One of the most interesting responses to the book (and to English classes in general) was given by Clare, an "A" student in Joy's course, as well as an "A" student since junior high school. When I talked with Clare, it became apparent that her sense of self as "A" student in many ways interfered with her considering any of the roles being offered. When asked to draw connections between parts of the course, Clare focused on the mechanics of course procedure, rather than on the ideas underlying the procedures:

> I never really think, I mean, is it supposed to tie together, I mean, I thought it was just part of the [laughs] English course. I mean you write papers you read books, and now we're ending them up and getting it all finished, you know, it's the end of the semester. (Final interview, spring 1986)

Clare was baffled by the questions—the course, to her, was just an English course. You read books, you wrote papers, and that was it. I asked her later if she saw a connection between her work and Laurence's. Even though Joy had written in response to one of her papers, "Do you realize how much like *Bird in the House* this is?" Clare denied seeing a connection:

> Maybe if I looked at it and she explained what she meant then I'd go "Oh." You know [laughs] but I don't—from what she wrote on my paper it said "did you notice how much this correlated with *Bird in the House*?" And I wrote about my childhood and how my old place where I used to live, in my mind subconsciously I think of it as a happy place because that's where my family was a whole, then we moved from there my sister [pause] went insane and my [pause] parents got divorced and [laughs] you know. And that's the only thing I wrote about and then she said that it correlates with *Bird in the House*, I don't, I don't know. [laughs] It's nothing like what happened in there. (Final interview, spring 1986)

Clare, much like Clark and Melody, could not see the connection between herself and Margaret Laurence. We can see a connection, though—her work describes family changes by focusing on a place, and it reflects on events that are hard to understand in family life. But because the plots are not similar, Clare could not see the connection even when it was pointed out. Later in her interview, she provided some reasons why she could not see the connection. Basically she said she had only read literature for "symbolism" in the past and was highly aware that she did not use symbolism as real writers do (thus she cannot be like Laurence). Secondly, she said writing classes should teach form—the forms for different types of essays will help students succeed in other classes. She said Joy helped with content but not form, and she could not see how writing personal stuff in this class would help her in her future history and business classes.

The roles for English classes that Clare posited are roles that are wholly connected to the school environment. From her past experience in classrooms, she "knew" what would be expected of her here and in the future. She already had a strong image of herself as someone who succeeds in English classes, writing formal papers and explicating the symbolism of literary works. She experienced Joy's course as an enjoyable break from such real work, but a break that was finally not worth her time.

In general, then, Clare never considered that writing could go on outside the school setting or that writing could be used to "explore and communicate" one's own life. Unlike Amy and Melody, who were excited to find Joy's course focusing on purpose rather than form, Clare was worried by it. It did not fit with her experience in other classrooms and therefore would not help her. For her, it appeared, the only role that mattered was the traditional role of good student. Neither the ADAPT student role nor the writer role offered in Joy's classroom fit with the role Clare expected. So, like a good student, she went through the course and did enough work to earn her "A," but she could not imagine being a writer or student in any context other than her past classrooms. In her refusal to consider such other possibilities lies her inability to see connections—and, of course, in her own mind she may be right. Joy's course very well may not help in future courses, if all one writes for is to satisfy course demands.

Underlife, Change, and Learning

Like the students in the audience-based class in chapter 3, what the students in this class learned was primarily a function of their identity negotiations. The ways they positioned themselves in relation to the available roles of student and writer determined their learning. Amy, Clark, and Melody all left the course exploring aspects of new writers' roles, considering ways that writing would help them in their future pursuits. Clare, on the other hand, left secure in her good student role, but unsure that the oddities of Joy's class would really help her behave as a good student in other classes. The students' negotiations with the available roles determined their sense of learning.

Unlike the students in the audience-based class, however, the students in Joy's class were able to explore their own relationships to writing, because the structure of the class made writers' roles available to them. Many students consequently described themselves as learning about writing. Because the course provided clearly defined writers' roles as alternatives to the student role of developing adolescent to diagnostician, students were able to explore writing as an activity which might have meaning outside the classroom. For most students, the presence of the writers' roles (as modeled by Joy through Margaret Laurence) allowed them to shift the context of their work from student-to-teacher to reflective writer in one's own world, and this shifted context led to a different sort of learning.

In their experience with Joy's course, many of the students thus paralleled Joy's own experience of change and underlife. Joy changed during the semester from contained to disruptive underlife, from an initial, troubled allegiance to the ADAPT program and its roles to the substitution of new purposes for her teaching with corresponding new roles. In working through her course, students similarly came to explore a difference between student writer roles and reflective writer roles. Their initial papers largely matched their past experiences of writing in English classes, but as the course went on the alternative role of reflective writer proved more and more important. Both teacher and students, in other words, found themselves shifting their work, their roles, and their perspectives on writing.

This shift, in many ways, is an underlife shift, experienced as an alternative to traditional school roles. For Joy as teacher, the change became explicitly a shift from contained to disruptive underlife, from minor dissatisfaction with her role to the creation of a new set of roles and purposes for her teaching. For the students, the shift was in general less dramatic: a feeling that alongside their behavior as students there were purposes for writing which would be important in contexts other than the classroom. When the students described their learning in the course, it was to these other purposes that they pointed. For example, Clark described the usefulness of audience awareness when speaking to others; Amy described the usefulness of writing to help her understand people.

The possibility of learning, it seems, is a function of such shifting roles. When students and teacher can move outside the limitations of traditional examinee-examiner roles, then kinds of learning become possible that were not possible before. Such a move, of course, is an underlife move relative to the existing educational system—a move more difficult for teachers (whose professional life is based in that system) than for students (who already are engaged in various forms of underlife towards student roles). In the course described in this chapter, we can see glimpses of the kinds of learning that such shifts in roles might allow in classrooms, for even in a course in transition students found alternative writers' roles compelling. In the next two chapters, we will see what kinds of learning are made possible when the consequences of the shift from student to writer roles are worked out more fully—in workshop environments.

5 A Writing Workshop and Emerging Writers' Identities

In the last two chapters, I have shown how students and teacher negotiate individual stances towards the roles available to them in classrooms. For students, this negotiation has conditioned the kind of learning they do, and for teachers, the kind of classes they teach. Taken together, the last two chapters present evidence that how and what students learn in writing classrooms can be described by their identity negotiations. Even in classes where role negotiation is seemingly not the focus, such negotiation still determines learning.

In this chapter, I will present evidence that learning to write depends on developing an understanding of the self as writer, and that workshop classes teach writing more effectively than other sorts of writing classes do by promoting such self-understanding. In describing a writing workshop class that Joy Ritchie taught in the spring of 1988, I will be focusing on the writers' roles the course made available, the ways in which students understood these roles, and the ways in which they connected these roles with their developing senses of self.

This shift in focus from teacher-student relationships (as in chapters 3 and 4) to writers' roles in the classroom is in many ways possible because of the nature of workshop courses. In the courses presented in the last two chapters, the driving structure was the temporal sequence of assignments given by the teacher. As they progressed through these courses, students found themselves writing according to the tempo of assignments and the conceptual sequence presented in the assignments. They wrote a paper or a revision each week, received teacher and student feedback, noted (or had explained) the underlying concepts that the exercise was intended to teach, and then went on to the next assigned task. Such a structure by its very nature encouraged students to focus on the concepts the teacher was presenting. The dominant role for them in the classroom was that of student, a role which required them to demonstrate their understanding of these concepts in the time the teacher allowed for each task.

In contrast, the driving structure of the workshop courses presented in this chapter and the next was quite different. Instead of a series of assignments (each with its underlying concepts and timetable), the workshop courses were organized around a sequence of predictable activities which students were encouraged to use in developing writings. Students in workshop courses know that finished work (work ready for its readers) will be due at midterms and finals, but until that time they are able to explore their developing pieces through a predictable sequence of exploratory writing and small group response. The focus of the course consequently shifts from grasping the concepts underlying teachers' assignments to deciding through practice how certain activities help or hinder one's own development of texts. This shift in focus, in and of itself, carries far-reaching consequences for how students learn and for the processes of identity negotiation, because it confronts students with a responsibility for their writing and learning which other classes do not.

In this chapter, I will describe the structure of the workshop course Joy Ritchie taught in 1988, the phases the class moved through in working with this structure, and the roles for writers and students this course presented. Then I will present several case studies of representative students' development in the course, focusing especially on the ways each student understood the course's roles for writers and negotiated a particular stance towards these roles.

The Course

Background: Writing Workshop Courses

Joy planned this course as an alternative to the course described in chapter 4 in an attempt to teach according to the principles which had become important to her. Rather than structure a writing course around a sequence of assignments promoting intellectual development, she intended to highlight students' own development as writers, their own agendas and purposes for writing, in a context that addressed questions of how and why writers actually write. These were the goals that had emerged as important during the semester described in chapter 4.

As a consequence of these new goals, Joy drew on her experience in Nebraska Writing Project workshops and her reading of college workshop teachers Peter Elbow and Donald Murray, and K–12 workshop teachers Lucy Calkins and Nancie Atwell. All of these sources supported a reorganization of writing classrooms around workshop principles, principles which emphasize the way learners learn writing (and other uses of language) according to their own tempos and not the tempos of school assignments. Although each of these sources offers somewhat different suggestions for teaching workshops, all agree on several important principles (summarized here from Nancie Atwell's *In the Middle*):

1. *Ownership:* "Writers need their own topics. Right from the first day of kindergarten students should use writing as a way to think about and give shape to their own ideas and concerns" (17).

2. *Predictable time spent on predictable activities:* "Writers need regular chunks of time—time to think, write, confer, read, change their minds, and write some more. Writers need time they can count on, so even when they aren't writing, they're anticipating the time they will be. Writers need time to write well" (17).

3. *Importance of response in many modes:* "Writers need response. Helpful response comes during—not after—the composing. It comes from the writer's peers and from the teacher, who consistently models the kinds of restatements and questions that help writers reflect on the content of their writing" (17).

4. *Presenting writing as a process:* "We need to write, share our writing with our students, and demonstrate what experienced writers do in the process of composing, letting our students see our own drafts in all their messiness and tentativeness" (18).

Principles like these underlie most forms of workshop teaching in this country. Joy's own experience in the Nebraska Writing Project (as student and teacher) had made her familiar with courses organized according to these principles.

Course Design and Teacher Rationale

In an interview the week before classes in the spring of 1988, Joy described her plans for her writing course. This semester, she explained, was the first chance she would have to do a writing course since the spring of 1986, and (following what she had learned from that semester) she intended this course to be a writing workshop. For her, this intention meant that she would set no assignments for student papers, but would instead let students work on topics of their own choice. Furthermore, except for due dates at midterms and finals, she would not set deadlines for student papers. Instead, she planned weekly group response sessions in which students would react to one another's work in progress. During these sessions, the authors would determine the kind of response they needed.

The plan for her course was as follows: Each week, all workshop participants would generate at least five pages of work in progress.

They would meet each Friday in small groups to discuss a selection of each group member's writing. These meetings would take two forms. On Fridays of odd weeks (weeks one, three, five, and so forth), everyone would bring work to read aloud to their small groups and get immediate oral feedback. On Wednesdays of even weeks, students would distribute photocopies of their work to their group with questions for written response, and on Friday of that week, students would discuss the written reactions to the piece. Mondays and Wednesdays would be spent in a variety of activities for developing ideas, discussing strategies, or reading excerpts from class members' work. At midterms and finals, portfolios of work from each student would be due for grading. The portfolios would contain finished pieces chosen by the individual and a process folder consisting of all unfinished work, all writing to overcome blocks or explore ideas, and all written responses to others' work. Participation in the workshop (that is, attendance, responsibility in bringing work to small groups, and participating in discussions) would also contribute to final grades.

This structure for the course had two important features. First, it was a predictable structure. Once students had worked through the first two or three weeks, they would know what to expect out of class activities and could begin planning to use this structure to accomplish tasks they set themselves. Second, it was a flexible, interactive structure. Joy had only planned the Monday and Wednesday activities for the first three weeks, realizing that after that point activities for those days depended a good deal on what students were writing and where they were with those writings. Depending on the tempo of their work, she expected to lead activities exploring invention, organization, revision, interviewing and other research strategies, and editing, but she could not predict ahead of time when these activities would be most relevant. Students could thus always predict the kind of activities which would occur in class, but Joy was also able to connect her Monday-Wednesday activities to students' developing needs as she perceived them.

The purpose for this predictable yet flexible structure was to allow the course to focus more directly on each individual student's development as a writer (the purpose which had emerged for her teaching in her last writing course). Joy put it this way in the introduction to her syllabus:

> This class is intended to help you develop your strengths as writers, to help you write more effectively for various audiences and purposes, and to give you greater confidence in your ability to read writing critically. In this class we will all be working writers, exploring the sources from which we can write—our own

experience, our reading, our observation of the world around us—
and we will be working to find ways of solving some of the
problems writers face as they develop their ideas and attempt to
present them to others. In the process, I hope you will experience
the satisfaction, pleasure and new insight writing can bring.

The course, then, would be a gathering of working writers exploring
what to write about, developing strategies for writing effectively, and
perhaps experiencing some of the pleasure and insight writing can
bring.

Phases in the Course

As the semester progressed, the course moved through three rather
distinct phases. During the first three weeks, Joy introduced the course
activities, modeling them herself (modeling phase). Then, from week
three until midterm papers were returned in week nine, Joy progressively
developed her sense of how writers behave, often in response to student
concerns or by embellishing things students themselves brought up
(role development phase). Finally, from week ten until the end of the
course in week fifteen, the course took on a weekly pattern of having
individuals discuss their work with the whole class Mondays and
Wednesdays, followed by small group meetings on Fridays (individual
readings phase). This pattern emerged because students were in such
radically different places with their work that no single set of activities
would meet even a high percentage of the students' needs. Discussions
of individual readings at least allowed them to take turns having their
work addressed.

Phase One: Modeling

In the first three weeks of class, Joy introduced students to how the
workshop would be conducted. She guided them through the major
activities of class by modeling them herself. She would do an invention
activity with students, bring in her draft the following day to show
how group meetings might work, and would lead discussions of student
readings to show what sort of responses she expected. In these activities,
she presented an initial image of what kinds of writing she valued and
what kinds of writerly behavior she expected in her workshop.

Each day of the first three weeks contributed to this modeling
process. The first day highlighted the various activities which would
become standard in the class: an activity was modeled, many students
had a chance to talk, and writing occurred. Joy handed out the syllabus,
explained it, then initiated an introduction exercise, which took the

rest of the hour. Individual students in the room interviewed someone they did not know, then wrote an introduction of that person, which they read to the class. In performing this exercise, everyone had a chance to speak and write, and each individual's past experience was to some degree made important.

On the second day, Joy followed up this introduction exercise with an activity she said was aimed at "the problem of what to write that all writers face." Borrowing an idea from Donald Murray's *A Writer Teaches Writing,* she had individual students make a list of things they were authorities on (by which she meant things they knew more about than most people). As students wrote their lists, she wrote her own list, suggesting sorts of topics aloud as she did so. The class then moved into a large circle, passed these lists around and wrote comments "explaining what interests you" on the list, and spent a little time talking to at least one person who had written on their lists.

For the last half hour of class, Joy had students freewrite about one of the topics or responses they had received and then asked volunteers to read their freewriting. Several students volunteered, and the class listened to initial writings which made fun of whining sisters, explained what a Husker Hostess does, stated what it felt like to be the only black person in class, and berated an anonymous responder for criticizing handwriting. Joy ended class by encouraging participants to work through these thoughts and responses to develop something they could write about. This class period served to introduce students to the kinds of activities they would experience on Mondays and Wednesdays during the course—activities would be presented as things they could use in their own various ways to help develop writings.

On the third day, modeling how she wanted small group meetings to proceed, Joy had the class do a sample response session on a draft she had written. She began by reminding everyone to bring a draft the next class for small groups, then explained her expectations for response. Drawing on (and recommending) Peter Elbow's chapters on feedback in *Writing with Power,* Joy explained a difference between criterion-based feedback (which compares a piece to certain accepted criteria for that kind of piece) and reader-based feedback (which describes what the individual, as reader, thought and felt as the piece was read). She stated that reader-based feedback is what she expected, because anyone can give such feedback without special training and because it can give writers insights into what happens in readers' heads. Using this mini-lesson as an introduction, Joy then wrote her rules for small group response on the board:

1. Writer speaks about writing, directing readers to the types of response she or he needs.
2. Readers respond to the questions and comments of the writer.
3. Writer follows up with further comments or directions.

This was the pattern that small groups were to follow in talking about each person's writing.

To make these expectations clear in practice, Joy had the class respond to a freewriting of hers. Her writing described her uncertainty about whether she should allow her thirteen-year-old son to read a sexually perverse science fiction book. After reading the piece, Joy asked students to avoid criterion feedback. Instead, she asked them for a sense of where she could head with this piece, what they thought her attitude towards the subject was, and where in the writing they identified her idea. Many students responded by focusing on censorship and parenting issues, and Joy redirected the response by explaining her own ambivalence towards both issues. The class talked about both the draft and their own feelings as teenagers who dealt with parents. Joy then dismissed class, reminding the students to bring drafts to read the next time.

In the fourth class period, Joy let students break up into groups of four or five and respond to each other's work. She wrote the "pattern for response" on the board again, then joined one group as a participating member (she had brought another draft of her own work). Groups worked by themselves until each person in the group had had a chance to read and be responded to, at which point they disbanded without handing in any work.

In the fifth class, Joy repeated the pattern of reading her own work to the class and having it responded to, but this time in the context of another "where we might find ideas" exercise. To begin class, she explained that we often find ideas by responding to things we read, even in places as simple as the newspaper. She then brought out an example. She read a piece from *Sports Illustrated* about a team of runners who ran as a centipede (all tied together) in the San Francisco marathon. After asking for student reactions and comments about this piece and topic, she read a response she had written to it, a response which began with her own experience as a solitary, noncompetitive runner and which developed into a reflection on our American value of rugged individualism as a potential problem. She asked for student response to this draft, using the small group pattern from the week before. Then she invited students to freewrite about any piece of writing they had recently read which might prompt a response, and she encouraged them to develop these thoughts into drafts for the next meeting.

In the sixth class, Joy invited students to read aloud the drafts they had written in response to writing. She let each volunteer read, then let the class react to the person's piece. In monitoring the reactions, she would ask individual reactors to explain why they reacted as they did, especially highlighting what in their experience or thinking made them react this way. This strategy effectively stopped any attempts to evaluate the piece and instead focused the class's attention on what happens inside various readers to prompt their reactions.

Interestingly, the students who read their work chose highly volatile subjects. They read about bullfighting, parents needing to be less worried about sexual promiscuity, and one young man's recovery from drug addiction. Especially during the response to this last topic, the class became very emotional because the volunteer was reading a true, personal piece. One young woman cried as she explained her response to it, saying that it made her think of her own inability to help a friend who was just beginning to experiment with drugs. At the end of class, Joy thanked the students for sharing, pointed out what a range of ideas for writing they had, and reminded them to bring copies of drafts for small groups the next class day.

On the seventh day, Joy prepared them for small group response by having them write out on their drafts the questions they wanted written response to and by having them summarize how they had written the draft—where the idea had come from, how long it had taken, what blocks they faced, and the like—as a tool for identifying what questions to ask. Then on the eighth day (now the third Friday of class), the same small groups met by themselves (Joy was again a member of one group), discussed their responses, and left when they had finished.

In the course of these three weeks, Joy presented the major activities and rules for the workshop by modeling the behaviors herself. Small group responses were modeled by responding to Joy's own drafts, but the groups were then left to work on their own. Activities for developing ideas for writing were tried in class as a whole, but individual writers were left to themselves to develop their own ideas. Individuals responded to public readings, but were encouraged to be explicit about why they responded as they did. A range of topics and styles of writing was presented by Joy and student volunteer readers. Taken together, all of these activities modeled how the workshop would proceed: individuals would work on topics and tasks which they themselves defined, in a context in which exploration activities, public readings, and small group responses would occur. These responses could be used or ignored as they fit into the development of individual pieces.

Phase Two: Role Development

The structure Joy had set up continued until midterms in week eight, when students turned in their first finished papers and their process folders for a grade. In this phase of the course, Joy's activities continued to emphasize and clarify her sense of how writers behave. She led the class through three more invention activities aimed at finding ideas for writing, three more days of discussing and modeling small group response strategies, two more days of discussing student volunteers' papers, a day of audience analysis, a day exploring revision strategies, and six small group meetings.

Throughout these activities, she continued to talk about and model her sense of writers at work: writers were people who wrote to explore what they thought and what they reacted to, who wrote to contribute to ongoing discussions about important social topics, who wrote for insight and the pleasure of accomplishment. In this phase her presentation of these writerly behaviors was supplemented and made more complex by several strong student voices in the classroom, voices which presented other versions of writers' roles. I will present some of the language Joy used to develop her writer's roles, then I will present some of the alternative voices which emerged during this time.

Joy's particular version of writer behavior can be traced in the language she used to describe writers' activity to the class. This language presented writers as people who use writing to explore or understand something in their world, often using this exploration to contribute to ongoing societal discussions of these topics. Furthermore, because writers are comfortable exploring ideas as well as expressing opinions, they are people who are reasonably tolerant of diversity—able at any rate to recognize diverse opinions and their own stance among them.

On the day following the class's first public reading, for example (in week three, when one student had cried and another had explained his drug addiction), Joy distributed an entry from her journal:

> I've thought a good bit about our class yesterday. Perhaps you've thought some about it also. It strikes me that we often ignore or don't take full account of relatively insignificant everyday occurrences like what goes on in class. In many respects our class Monday was like many other classes—people brought up interesting ideas and we talked about them with some interest and engagement. And then we all left and went about the rest of our business. But as writers I think we need to give more thought to

what happened in class. By writing their careful, genuine, thoughtful responses to something they had read, Rachel, George, Bob
and Gwen made some important personal discoveries, and their
writing made some sort of impact, touched a small but vital nerve
in most all of us. They each led us to reflect for at least a few
minutes about some of the most essential human questions and
problems. That's one of the most important things writers do.
But we'll each have to decide what use, if any, we choose to make
or can make of the ideas they presented, how we might transform
them into problems or ideas we'd like to pursue in our own
writing. . . . My point is simply to re-emphasize that we have a
lot of possibilities for writing very near at hand. But unless we
take time to pursue them, to try them out, we won't be able to
do much with those ideas. I want to provide you with some time
to do that in class, but I encourage you to try to find time to do
some informal, speculative writing outside of class. Most writers
keep a journal or notebook in which they record their observations
and reflections. If you haven't ever done that, I'd like to encourage
you to try it.

This response to the class highlighted many aspects of the writer
role as Joy understood it. It focused on the many subjects for writing
"near at hand" if writers made the time for "informal, speculative
writing." It focused on the way writers in this classroom had used their
response to reading to make "important personal discoveries" and to
"touch a small vital nerve" in listeners. It focused explicitly on the
differences between the rather simple classroom context in which their
writing occurred and the wider, more complicated context in which
their writing might occur. Students were invited, though not assigned,
to explore these roles further.

Joy's activities during these weeks highlighted these aspects of writers'
behavior. For those who were having trouble coming up with ideas,
she presented reflective activities like describing beliefs they had changed
in their lives or reconsidering a position they held after talking with
someone who believed something else. She highlighted the social nature
of writing by leading a week-long set of activities focused on writing
as conflict resolution—how it can help individuals clarify their position
on a conflict, how certain strategies are more likely than others to
invite dialogue if one has to write to a hostile audience. And she
repeatedly asked individuals to read their texts to the whole class,
guiding the ensuing class discussions by focusing on the different
responses individuals had and reasons for those responses. The image
of writing as a reflective and expressive act, occurring within a pluralistic
social context, was repeatedly presented by these activities.

Following midterms, Joy's summary of class writings likewise highlighted these writers' roles. Rather than address grades and performance,

her class handout presented "a list of some of the ideas people have been working on thus far," since "with seven weeks left in the semester, some people seem to know what they want to work on, other people want to take a breath and come up for air to look for new ideas." This handout presented two unordered lists. One list, entitled "Exploring what has made a difference in my life, influences, how I've changed and am changing," included such topics as "Growing up Catholic," "Coming of age in the sixties," "Surviving the first freshman semester," "Living as a minority student in white culture," and "Coping with cancer." The second list, entitled "Exploring ideas and issues," included "Racism at UN-L," "Losses and gains in love relationships," and "Why isn't education in our country working." Such a presentation of midterm work focused attention again on reflection about lived experience and on contribution to ongoing discussion of issues within a pluralistic society.

Joy, in short, used her class activities and her written responses to student work to highlight what was important for her about writers' behavior and about the role of writer in our culture. In this phase of the course, her own behavior, activities, and responses modeled and developed these aspects of the writers' roles.

But Joy's version of writers' roles was not the only version presented in the classroom during this phase. Because of the number of opportunities for students to talk (and even lead discussion), certain students were able to present their own versions of writers' roles relatively forcefully. Although there were many writers' roles suggested in passing, two of these became particularly powerful in classroom dynamics: the role of writer as inspired genius, and the role of publishing creative writer.

The role of writer as inspired genius was consistently raised in class by Bob, the young man who wrote about recovering from LSD. Often when revision or process was brought up, he raised his hand and said that his first draft was always his final draft, because he felt writing should "capture the moment" in which it was written and revising a piece somehow violated this process. He said he would rather write an entirely new piece than rewrite an old one. Because he frequently volunteered to read his work in class during these weeks, his was an important alternative voice to Joy's. Bob was, at this point in the semester, generating a vast amount of writing, all of it interesting if not polished, and hence his claim functioned as an alternative claim about writers' behavior.

The other alternative role of writer as publishing creative writer was advocated by Lillian, a junior English-economics double major. Very early in the course, she began leading her small group in longer and longer discussions of their writing—in some ways being even more thorough in discussion than Joy was. On days after group meetings when Joy would ask groups to summarize their discussions, Lillian and her group members, Charles and Mark, were always the first to respond and the ones who talked the most. They consistently articulated insights about their writing and their group response. Consequently, they presented the class with a "model" of a committed, writerly small group in operation. (In fact, in private interviews several students told me they wished they were in Lillian's small group because it seemed so committed to writing.)

The reason Lillian's group always had things to say, always took longer in meetings than other groups, and dominated class discussion about response was that Lillian's personal goal for the semester was to produce publishable creative writing. On the day before midterms were due, for example, Joy asked each small group to generate a list of criteria on which they wanted her to grade their work. Where most groups came up with relatively standard lists of organization, clarity, originality, and correctness, Lillian's group suggested the following:

> Hard-core criterion: Is it publishable?
>
> Complete? Self-contained?
>
> Is it crap? Worth reading?
>
> Teach, delight, move you?

Once each group's criteria had been placed on the board, it was on Lillian's list that students focused. Lillian and Charles explicitly told Joy that she had been "too nice" and "they didn't want niceness." Other students expressed doubts about their work as publishable, and Lillian confronted the class, asking, "Am I the only one who sees publication as a goal?" Silence ensued, till finally Mark said, "Maybe not right now, but in the future." Several other students then agreed that "maybe not publishable, but better than a class paper" was a reasonable way of setting the criteria.

Lillian's forceful agenda for her own writing thus raised the class's general sense of commitment or seriousness about writing—or at least presented a model of someone other than the teacher who was committed to publishable writing. Because of her focus on publication, Lillian's role of writer was more forceful than the role Joy presented, since the harsh reality of submission costs and rejection letters was an issue. Because of Bob's and Lillian's voices, consequently, the writers' roles which developed in Joy's classroom were not merely the ones Joy presented. Instead, a range of writers' roles emerged in the workshop, and students needed to negotiate their positions amid this range.

Phase Three: Individual Readings

Following midterms, the class entered its third and last phase. With the workshop pattern and the various roles for writers fairly well developed, students had approximately five weeks in which to finish their work for final evaluation. Reflecting on her students, Joy said that she had been surprised at midterms to find just how many different places they were in and felt very unsure about what to do with the remaining time. She explained:

> Two days ago, what was most on my mind was what in hell am I going to do for the next four weeks? Now it's worrying that they aren't where I thought they'd be—needing to remind myself that all students aren't Lillian, but second semester freshmen— need more hands-on work with papers instead of just talk about these processes. This is tricky and will require keeping up with the reading of papers, and I need to overcome some reluctance to read and have their papers worked on in class. (Interview notes, March 1988)

She realized that at this point she could hold "no global vision" about the class, but instead had "individual agendas for each student." Consequently, during Mondays and Wednesdays of the last four weeks, Joy invited different students to read their work aloud and guide the whole class in a response session. More than half of the class took this opportunity. The students began what was essentially a turn-taking series of response sessions in which individuals took turns having their work discussed.

Joy had some misgivings about this way of ending the course. She said in her final interview that she was not at all sure this series of sessions was what everyone needed. But she also pointed out that, given what she knew about each student, she "would have to be three more people" to give them all what they needed, but "on the other hand if they can work with each other then they don't need me as much." She explained:

> I'm seeing the workshop as an enormously complex scenario with multiple actors, fluctuating scenes, multiple values and motives, all intersecting like a complicated geometric pattern. I'm realizing I'm only one small piece of drama going on, I'm not entirely the director, or maybe just a director with limited power—the actors bring a lot from themselves to the drama. I'm thinking a lot about the nature of classroom communities: what creates com-

munity is a sense of reciprocal influence, when a majority feel
their acts have meaningful influence on people. A workshop
should allow other people to have meaningful influence on each
other, more varied group dynamic patterns, not all communication
lines through teachers. I'm seeing this in my class, in Shandra's
paper [on being black in white culture] sparking other papers, in
Lillian's sense of self as writer affecting Mark and Charles.
(Interview notes, March 1988)

Joy sensed that the workshop had created a context where students
were learning in a variety of different ways—and consequently focusing
on a variety of different writing topics and problems. She could not
meet all their different needs as developing writers, but then no context
could. What was happening, though, was a kind of mutual influence,
a kind of workshop where students were influencing each other instead
of always relying on the teacher. Ending her course with a series of
individual response sessions was consequently in keeping with what
was happening.

Roles for Students and Writers

Joy's workshop course, unlike the courses described in the last two
chapters, presented students with more possible roles as writers than
as students. The student role, as one student put it, was an "easy" role
to figure out: the contract about what determined grades was clear.
Writers' roles, on the other hand, were more diverse.

1. *Student role:* From the very beginning of class, it was recognized
that to be a good student, individuals had to attend the class meetings,
meet deadlines, participate in group discussions, write five pages per
week, and at the end of the fifteen weeks turn in 20 to 25 pages of
writing they had finished during the semester. These were reasonably
straightforward criteria, perceived as easy to achieve. Shandra, a "B+"
student at midterms, told me in an interview that the course seemed
easier to her than some other writing courses—in fact it even seemed
to her that "getting grades" and "improving writing" were somewhat
opposed because she could get good grades without working hard. Tim,
a "C" student at midterms, echoed Shandra's sense of clarity in
evaluation. He had expected his grade, he said, and "knew why" he
had received it. He simply and plainly had not been doing the five
pages of writing per week that was part of the contract.

2. *Writers' roles:* Because of the interaction in the workshop, at
least three roles for writers were prevalent. One role was that presented
by Joy herself. She presented writers as people who (a) use writing

reflectively, to explore and understand experience; (b) use writing to communicate their explorations, aware that the community in which they express their opinions is diverse; and (c) are tolerant, being able to listen and reflect on the views of other people. The other roles were presented by students. Bob argued for and modeled a role of writer as inspired genius, and Lillian motivated and provoked the class with her role as publishing writer.

It was to the complexity of these writers' roles that most students reacted in placing themselves in the course. The workshop classroom allowed most of students' identity negotiations to focus on their relationship to the possible writers' roles as opposed to a great concern with the role of student. In the second half of this chapter, I will describe several students' reactions to the class, with particular emphasis on how they negotiated their positions amid these offered roles.

Student Response

As they did in the course described in the last chapter, students responded to Joy's class in overwhelmingly positive fashion on the department's student evaluations. Almost all students rated the course and instructor "excellent."

Unlike the last class, however, all of the ten students I interviewed throughout the semester thought they had improved as writers, and eight of these students, in part as a response to the class, saw themselves going on to (or at least exploring) professions where writing would be an important part of their lives. The students as a group left articulating an understanding of themselves as writers in some new fashion.

Of course, students understood themselves as writers in different ways, depending on their own negotiations among available roles. Among the students I interviewed, two general patterns of negotiation occurred. One group of students already seemed to think of themselves as writers when they entered the course; for them, their experience in the course helped to clarify what it meant for them to be a writer. A second group of students entered the course thinking of themselves as students but not necessarily as writers; these students began to articulate a role for themselves as writers which they might explore in the future. In the section that follows, I will present examples of both patterns of response.

Pattern One: Clarifying One's Role as Writer

Several students entered this class with an already developed sense of themselves as writers. For them, the class largely served as an environment where they could explore that sense of self in relation to the writers' roles presented by Joy and other students. Depending on the roles with which they entered class and their particular negotiations during class, these students clarified their roles in particular ways. Of the ten students I interviewed, four exhibited this pattern of response. The responses of two of these students, Bob and Gwen, will illustrate the point.

Bob

By his own admission, Bob entered class as a good writer but a poor student. Throughout class, his interest in his own ability and performance as writer remained high, but, as he predicted, he struggled with his general resistance to student roles (and other roles which, in his words, forced expectations on him). At the beginning of the course, he argued forcefully for a role of writer as an imaginative, inspired person, more creative and hence superior to others. By the end of the course, he still saw himself as a superior writer, but he said he found new importance in recognizing how other people view his work and revising to influence their vision.

Bob's desire to be thought of as a superior writer and resistant student was clear in much of his behavior during the first half of the semester. During my first interview with him (three weeks into the semester), he explained that "writing and commercial art are the best stuff I do" and that he was "a better writer than most people," writing music, poetry, and stories in addition to his schoolwork. He also explained that he was on academic probation this semester and had switched from journalism to advertising because his grade-point average was lower than that required by journalism. He complained about all the "fraternity bullshit" his fraternity made him do (especially the grades they required for activation), but also bragged that he was doing all the writing for two of his fraternity brothers' classes as well as his own. All of these statements show that Bob had a strong opinion of himself as writer and a rather low opinion of structured roles like those of his classes and his fraternity house.

These perceptions of himself were evident in Bob's classroom behavior. In the first few weeks, he was very vocal in class. Whenever the class was asked for reactions, he volunteered and usually tried to tell several related stories. When Joy would quiet him and ask someone else to speak, he would talk to the person next to him, rattle his desk, look out the window. On small group days, he dominated his group's discussion, often taking more than his share of time to tell stories about ideas he had for writing. When Joy brought up revision in class, Bob argued with her, presenting his image of writing as something that "captures the moment of creation" and should not be revised. In the third-week interview, when I asked him if he was aware he was struggling with Joy for control of the floor, he said that he had a history of this in classrooms, was aware of it, but "caught himself this time and would try to limit it." In his early class behavior, Bob was resisting his role as student and promoting his role as superior, creative writer very forcefully.

By midterms, Bob's responses to class had shifted somewhat. He was still resisting student roles, but doing so now by skipping class about once a week and falling behind on his writing. Two new reactions to class had begun to affect him, however. One was a reaction to how others were responding to his work:

> I feel totally isolated, was mad at the whole class one time (but felt I was stupid afterwards). I read a paper, they didn't respond, so I stopped talking in class. I really don't feel anybody sees where my writing comes from, probably because everybody writes on reactions to important things. They don't use stories from their own minds, and I'm getting bored with what they write— I'm waiting for "writing for fun" writing, not "poke your head and make you think" stuff. If I wanted that, I could watch Sixty Minutes.

Because the workshop allowed considerable opportunity for various people to respond to writing, Bob had become aware that how he saw his writing was not how others saw it, that there was a gap in communication. At midterms, he felt isolated from the other students because of this. He was also resisting Joy's attempts to model reflective writer behavior, writing "to poke your head and make you think."

But at the same time, Bob had been impressed by some of the writing others had read and said he had developed a new goal for the course:

> I want to write something *good,* something that everybody can sit back and go "that's all right"—I don't care if it gets published or is spectacular, just something that I can feel really good about.

This new goal was partly in response to other students, but mostly in response to Joy. As he put it,

> Joy does have individual goals for different people. She wants me to write a "knock your socks off" type deal—because she liked in my notebook just about everything I've written, she's looking for one thing to stand out from everything else. Her class is harder than my roommate's class with really strict assignments. Joy makes you think for yourself, she expects you to think a lot about

what you write, to put a lot of time into it, and then polish it. I
think these are good expectations.

By midterms, Bob had decided that he wanted to write one impressive
piece and was beginning to see (through all the reactions to his writing)
that with thinking and time and revision he might accomplish this.
His desire for others to be impressed with his writing, coupled with
the fact that their current reactions were not what he wanted, was
leading him to consider trying some of the things Joy modeled.

When Bob finished the course, his stance towards student roles and
writer roles was still tumultuous. When I interviewed him during finals
week, he had dropped further behind in Joy's course and had been
suspended from his fraternity house for getting into a fight. But he had
succeeded in earning two fraternity brothers "Bs" in their writing
courses and was excited about the possibility of writing a book over
the summer. His enduring resistance to student roles and his feelings
of superiority as writer clearly remained intact.

But Bob's stance towards revision and group work had changed
dramatically. As he put it,

> I will use peer feedback a lot. I like that, I like getting what they
> think. I'll probably always do that. I didn't really do this before
> this class, I'd just write stuff and hand it in. I can see now what
> others are seeing in my drafts, seeing what I need to do with
> them. I feel my writing has come around to being less jumbled,
> less "does this make sense to anybody but me?"—reading the
> stuff to class has really shown where it doesn't make sense.

Through his course experience, Bob discovered that readers have reasons
for how they respond to writing and that, with work, he can control
their responses better by revising, especially after sharing a piece with
several readers. Even with his initial resistance to revising and his sense
of isolation midway through the course, this experience was important
for him. "Class," he said, "really shaped my writing instead of forcing
it into a certain form—it was meant to shape what you wrote, not
drastically change it." Bob felt it was a great class for these reasons and
left accepting that while he would probably get a "C" grade, "it was
my fault, I didn't put enough in." He said he hoped to take as many
writing classes as he could in the future; he had already signed up for
a film and television writing class.

In the course of the semester, although Bob maintained his resistant
relationship to student roles and his strong sense of himself as writer,
he clarified his understanding of how writers behave and write. The
many opportunities for response to his work allowed him to see that
readers were not just being petty or dull in their response, but instead

that his work did not emerge perfectly formed in first drafts. Hence he added to his sense of writers' behavior the necessity of revision and response and praised his class experience because of this. His understanding of writing had improved during the class. Already seeing himself as a superior writer, Bob added this new understanding to his sense of being a writer.

Gwen

Like Bob, Gwen saw herself as a good writer when she entered the course. She was enrolled in the journalism college and had worked as a journalist in high school. Unlike Bob, she did not find it difficult to fulfill student roles, and she did not resist in the same ways he did. Nor did she resist the ideas of revision and response as Bob had. Instead, her progress through the course was one of exploring new options for writing. She spoke repeatedly in interviews of a contrast between journalistic writing and the writing Joy was encouraging. Initially, she just noted this contrast, but by the end of the course she had decided these new possibilities for writing were things she could use to improve her journalistic writing, as well as things worth doing for their own sake.

In my first interview with Gwen (three weeks into the course), she explained that she had declared a news editorial major and was hoping to make good grades so that she would be admitted to the journalism college. She expected a career in news editorial writing, but thought she might have to start doing copyediting and layout after college. She occasionally wrote stories and poems for her own enjoyment and occasionally wrote in a journal, but was not at all sure she would keep those activities up. In other words, when she entered class Gwen was focused on journalistic writing as a career and had a sense of herself as a developing journalist. She did some other kinds of writing, but did not at all see them as central.

Gwen did, however, claim to "really like" Joy's class already. As she put it, the class was "free, as opposed to the assigned topics of her last class," and Joy's agenda was

> how to become a better writer, what kinds of things go into different types of pieces, the atmosphere you write in—basically independence, everyone in class is an individual, everyone writes differently, a different style, and that's good.

Gwen perceived the context of the class as a place where she could work on her own writing and welcomed the possibility.

By midterms, Gwen had used some of Joy's exploration activities to develop one paper about her reactions to the Vietnam War and another paper about a friend who had cancer. She was writing about five pages a week and had tried out but abandoned a number of different topics. In my second interview with her, she wanted to talk directly about her potential as a writer and a desire that Joy push her even harder:

> Joy wants us to learn what potential you have as writer, to improve skills that you have. Obviously, some are more talented than others, but more practice also makes you better. She wants me to learn that I can write just as good as anyone else if I only work at it. I feel she should push me to be a better writer. I'm going to be a journalist, what I'm working on now (personal feeling stories, fiction) will help in writing news stories well. The writing I'm doing for Joy will help me be a better well-rounded person in terms of knowing the range of writing available, as well as a better journalist.

At midterms, Gwen had reflected on personal writing (reactions, fiction) in contrast to journalistic writing and now thought they enhance each other. Doing the personal writing, she thought, made her a "better well-rounded person" and "a better journalist." She had found that much of the writing she had initially thought was not part of her career might actually be.

Gwen continued this progression towards confidence and an expanded writer's role in her final interview, conducted the week before finals. Since midterms, she had finished her pieces on Vietnam and her friend with cancer and had also written a short story. She claimed this was "the best work I've done for a long time," and explained:

> I'm satisfied. Never had a class where you do so many things. It expanded my outlook. Such a variety of things we do, I never realized I could do all of it. I did fiction, personal experience I did a lot of that, reactions to world events. . . . In the past, my work hasn't been great, it's been journalism. "Get out the story fast," and this is more "sort out your thoughts." A big pace difference, had more time, that's helped a lot. I've done a lot of revision in the time I had. When you go fast in journalism, it's just basic facts, when you have more time you get more creative and more detailed.

Gwen started out thinking of herself as a journalistic writer and left thinking of herself as possessing potential she had not explored before. In her potential as a writer, journalism was just one kind of writing, a "fast" kind of writing focusing on "getting the story out quick." In this class, she had explored another kind of writing, writing at a slower pace that allowed reflection and creativity.

Her experience, Gwen said, would affect her future work:

> In future classes, I'll have a way of pacing myself to write, to get
> something out every week, have lots of stories to draw ideas
> from. I will do class assignments and will keep private notebooks
> which may or may not help in class, but I'll use this kind of
> writing [reflective writing] in both really. . . . My writing is becom-
> ing less formal, starting different things, trying a variety, I'm still
> figuring out what I'm best at. I'm taking fiction writing next year,
> and I'd still like to write a column.

She had found uses for the reflective and personal writing Joy was
presenting. Gwen was no longer sure that she would limit herself to
"just journalism," but instead was going to explore fiction writing and
private notebook writing. Thus she had formed a richer sense of her
potential as a writer, of the range of things she might do. While she
still thought of herself primarily as a journalist, she now saw other
options which served other purposes, but which were also attractive.

Gwen uncovered these other options, she said, because of the way
the class allowed her to develop her own agenda. As she put it:

> I think she teaches independence in writing. She doesn't set down
> something in front of you, it's what you want to do. Makes you
> develop your own style, your own type of writing. This is her
> agenda. It ends up seeming that everybody has a different agenda,
> we do stuff to help people each day, and in a sense it ends up
> with everybody having their own.

When Gwen perceived herself as allowed to work on her own agenda,
she discovered areas of her behavior as a writer that attracted her. She
hoped to explore them in the future, in and out of classes, as she
continued her journalist training. She had clarified and enriched her
sense of what a writer does and who a writer is during the course of
the workshop.

Pattern Two: Exploring the Possibility of a Writer's Role

For Gwen and Bob, the course provided an opportunity to clarify what
it would mean for each of them to be a writer. For many other students
who were not sure they wanted to be writers, the course provided
something much more modest: a chance to explore, in a reasonably
safe setting, some writerly behavior and to see whether or not such
behavior might have a place in their lives. Given that most of the
students in Joy's class were in the second semester of their first year,
this more modest opportunity was what most students reacted to. Tim
and Charles are illustrative of this pattern.

Tim

A fourth-semester sophomore majoring in social work, Tim entered the class doubting that he would ever do much writing. He had already been in college three years (a year's worth of "Ds" from a smaller college did not transfer), and he already knew what the hospital social work job he wanted would be like. For this job, Tim told me in his first interview, he would only have to write in a "business format" to fill out forms and make notes; his primary work would be oral. He was only taking the course because it was a requirement. Tim, in other words, saw himself on entering class as a nonwriter, someone who would endure through class only because he had to. His experience in class was much colored by his sense of self as nonwriter, but in time he came to explore the possibility of some aspects of writing. Joy's course confronted him and then led him to consider a certain kind of "therapy writing," as he called it, which proved more useful than he had expected.

As an experienced college student, Tim had "shopped around" before taking this course, sitting in on the first week of several writing classes before signing up for this one. In his first interview with me (four weeks into the semester), Tim explained that he had liked the "authority list activity" and the "therapy stuff" that others were writing, and this is what had attracted him to the class:

> I wanted to write on my own topics, and I like the therapy stuff, the papers of drugs and rapes and suicide. It's neat to know that others are doing this, although I don't see myself writing these papers.

Early on, Tim was attracted to the serious writing other students were doing—Eva's writing about being blind, Shandra's writing about being black, Bob's paper on drug addiction—papers like these interested Tim and intrigued him. "No one besides me is afraid to write what they feel," he said, reflecting on his classmates. He himself kept to relatively safe topics: his first paper was on beekeeping, something his family had done for years.

By midterm week, Tim's interest in "therapy writing" had prompted him to start a draft of a paper on why he wanted to do social work, a draft he showed Joy in his notebook. He felt profoundly ambivalent about this writing:

> Joy has different goals for different people. She wants me to write stuff I don't want to write, "therapy" stuff, experiences, like suicide for example. I don't want to express feeling or emotion, don't think I could write in detail a good four or five page paper. It

would be hard to express, and I wouldn't want anyone else to know. Joy wants us to feel okay writing about anything, so once we write it we won't think it's that tough. I haven't met her expectations, I'm not writing those kinds of papers. Like this social work paper, I will write this, but I don't want to share it with anyone. . . . I feel like I'm leading up to that social work paper—suicide, social work, it all has to deal with the same thing, an episode in my past. I feel like I'm going to the dentist: something painful, but I'll be better for it.

Tim felt a set of contradictory desires. He was attracted to the therapy writing he saw going on in class, writing which reflected on and made sense of past experience, and had begun to try it himself. But he also was resisting this writing, feeling that he was being pushed into it by Joy and that he wanted to avoid it. He knew he needed to do more work (he had not done as well at midterms as he wanted to do, primarily because he had not done enough writing), but he was not sure he wanted to do that work.

Between midterms and finals, Tim did write his social work paper, but he never read it to the class. Instead, he read aloud a paper on "Why the Greek System Is a Good Thing" when it was his turn to have the class discuss his work. Class discussion in response to this paper was lively—Greeks and "God Damn Independents" explained the stereotypes each had of the other, the problems they had with each other's values, the past experiences which led them to these reactions. Tim was shocked by this response and said he "felt like crawling into a hole" after the discussion. He had not considered that something uncontroversial for him would spark such intense reactions from different people. "I just abandoned that paper," he said. "I'm really aware of a pervasive Greek/Independent split as I leave class."

Perhaps as a response to having his worst fears about response confirmed in this reading (people would indeed understand him in different ways, and some would judge him badly because of what he wrote), Tim then went ahead and finished his social work paper. In his final interview, he explained that this paper had been a success:

It's hard for me to figure out real reasons, like in my social work paper, hard because I haven't thought it all out, still in process of thinking. . . . I used my social work paper in writing a five page self-description for applying for the social work program [at another school].

He had finished the paper, recognized how hard it was to do "that kind" of reflective thinking, but had found it useful. Since he had immediately used the paper in his program application, he thought the paper "would be the only one he'd ever use." Reflecting on the paper led him to identify what he had learned and how he had learned it:

> Revising is a big thing, she's taught me make my papers longer, more exact. I feel I can do that on my own now. . . . I liked the way she planned it, like, I got stuff out of Shandra's paper, a lot of people got stuff off of people reading their papers in class. I did: ways to start papers, makes us feel okay to write about anything, don't be afraid to write something. This is the biggest thing I got from all that was read in class.

At the end of class, Tim could see how the course had helped him overcome a fear of writing about personal topics and could see how his own writing about social work had helped him write an application and figure out how to revise. He recognized that this experience was a consequence of all the oral reading of papers that students did in class. Through this reading he learned that there was really nothing to fear. For him, this was an insight, and even though he would "never take another writing class" because he had fulfilled that college requirement, he left realizing that the class had helped him overcome this fear:

> In my case, this [class] got my social work paper out, probably the hardest paper I've ever had to write. . . . I've progressively put more time into this class, enjoyed it more, I'd recommend it.

Throughout the semester, Tim had explored the role of reflective writer that Joy was presenting. By and large he ignored the other writer's roles because he was attracted only to reflecting on his past and had no desire to be a publishing or inspired writer. By the time Tim left the course, he had worked through a fair amount of attraction-repulsion feelings about reflective writing and had written the "hardest paper ever." He left not to become a writer in any public sense, but with a bit more understanding of writing as a reflective activity. He had been able to try out one aspect of writerly behavior that intrigued and scared him, and now he knew that he "didn't have to be afraid" of such writing.

Charles

In contrast to the students described so far, Charles had expected and wanted a traditional, teacher-controlled writing class. Because he had done well in college before, especially when teachers set forth fairly rigid assignments, he found himself challenged and uncertain about the workshop atmosphere of Joy's course. Throughout the course, Charles struggled to understand "what this course was teaching him" and struggled with his own performance, since that performance did not match his earlier college successes. He ended up deciding that he was learning something far more central and important in this class, something he really needed to learn about how to be a writer. His struggles with the roles of the classroom thus led to a reinterpretation of the importance of those roles in his life.

During my first interview with Charles (three weeks into the course), he explained his expectations for the course and the stress he was experiencing:

> I like the open nature of class but I also feel uncomfortable. I have a desire for control in classes, I feel like nurturing teaching is important, but I'm ambivalent, uncomfortable. It can get taken advantage of somehow. I expected a textbook, but I'm not sure what to make of that. I feel comfortable writing in and out of class for Joy, but I want a book of rules.

Unlike other students, Charles was a junior, had already taken a lot of English classes, and had done well enough to be considering graduate school (although he was not sure in what area). All his other English courses had had explicit instructions and assignments for papers. He was not getting this, and felt ambivalent about it.

The reason Charles did not just reject the course, given his expectations, was that some of his own goals for writing seemed to connect directly with Joy's. He perceived himself as someone who was very interested in "the power of words and how people use them," but as someone who "had problems writing stuff down." For this reason he was taking the course as a supplement to the college's writing requirement. Consequently, Joy's focus on process and response impressed him:

> Communicating seems to be really important to her, and to me. . . . I find my own writing is so often a cover up for what I'm trying to say. This course will help me, understanding what I'm trying to say rather than clear stuff—I remember being a youth counselor in high school, I try to understand so hard that I make too many judgments and assumptions. I felt really comfortable the day we responded to writing, I feel comfortable reacting to her writing. . . . I felt comfortable getting criticism from them.

Charles perceived himself as someone who recognized the power of language and was fascinated by it. He also thought of himself as someone who had trouble saying or writing what he meant, sometimes even knowing what he thought, and found himself mulling over words and experiences, trying to get at what lay behind them. The role of writer as reflective thinker, as Joy presented it, was consequently something he was immediately attracted to. It matched his own tendency to circle back over experience in language.

In class, Charles was a member of Lillian's small group. During the first eight weeks, he managed to write part of an essay and an interior monologue sketch of a bus ride he had taken. Lillian and Mark responded to these drafts with intensity, but also shared with him the growing volumes of material they were producing (Lillian herself brought more than forty pages to small group during this time). By midterms, Charles was very aware that he was different from his group members, but he was also attracted to them:

> Lillian intimidated me at first, a really get up and go person, no roots, great grades, dollars for grad school—the kind of person I'd like to be but am not—now I'm very comfortable, I walk her home, get together outside of class to go over papers. I admire her writing, don't admire some of her goals in life. She's got intensity I'm attracted to. Mark is more level-headed than Lillian, but also intense, disciplined, a nose to the grindstone guy. So he's like Lillian there, but different also.

This small group had yet another influence on Charles. Where he had originally expected a "do the assignment" course and had stayed in it because he liked Joy's focus on response and reflection, he now had to contend with Lillian's role of publishing writer and the level of commitment this implied. Lillian's and Mark's commitment to writing allowed him to articulate a clear difference between how they acted as writers and how he had acted in his past classes:

> I'm not being realistic with myself, no one just sits down and writes great stuff right out. I'm writing more than I ever have, for example I only wrote eighteen pages all semester in last class, so I think I'm getting better. . . . But I don't know. I can't write, I'm displeased with almost everything I write. I can't discipline myself to sit down and write. I can do *assigned* writing on *assigned* topics in Renaissance Literature easily, but the self-sponsored writing is tough. But I *knew* this about myself before I took this class, it's why I took it.

At midterms, there was a clear difference in Charles's mind between "assigned" writing (which he did well) and "self-sponsored writing" (which Lillian and Mark did well, though Mark struggled). This difference was now one which Charles could explain to himself: he could even claim he took this class because of it. But he was still ambivalent—the role of writer as self-sponsored, reflective thinker conflicted with his acknowledged ability to be a good student:

> I thought I wanted a composition crutch, something to lean on. [Joy's] not going to give us that. Her expectations are that we have to learn on our own, on our internals. This may actually be better, but it's hard to say without having had the class I expected. I feel like not having the crutch is why I'm stalling, nothing to tell me how to do it. It's not meeting my expectations for how a course operates, but it's teaching me stuff I need to know. You kind of become your own teacher in a way, and group is a kind of teacher. I'm on the fence about this course, I'll see where it goes.

Charles was suspended amid the roles surrounding him: the student writer following rules from his past, the reflective writer Joy modeled, the publishing writer Lillian modeled. All attracted him in some ways and threatened him in others. Some he felt good about, others he did not. At midterms, he was unsure what to do with this situation, unsure where he fit and how he evaluated the many writers' roles.

Between midterms and the end of the course, Charles continued to attend class but basically gave up writing. He took part in groups, responded to writing in class, but fell further and further behind in his own work. In terms of his initial goals to do well as a student, Charles had done poorly in the class, something he noted in his final interview by comparing himself with Lillian:

> I think my work was pretty bad. I set out to do a lot of writing and I didn't end up doing that much. Not really sure why I didn't, maybe I had a goal without a path to that goal. So I didn't set out on the path and hence didn't achieve the goal. All goal, no how to get there. This is in contrast to Lillian: she plots out every week, every day, she'd get something there.

Charles told me he expected a "D" in the class. But he did not focus on this lack of success, because something far more important had happened to him:

> Oh really, I'm not frustrated because I think things are changing. I've come to an obstacle I've always avoided before, and now I'm face-to-face with it. I see that as positive. I'm making plans to change it, I think they will really change. I feel comfortable, ready to keep going. I just have to make a commitment, something I've never done before. . . . You know, my past experiences in writing compositions were to go to the library, get criticisms, and sort of find stuff I support to write out. I've always leaned on something, and in here I'm on my own. . . . What I need is not to learn anything more, I just need to do it, if I can't do it myself there's not a teacher who can make me.

Charles described coming face to face with an obstacle he had not seen before, an obstacle involving commitment. The course had allowed him to see this problem because it was not just an "assignment" course, a "crutch" course. Instead, he was on his own. In watching himself behave in comparison with Lillian and Mark, he had figured out what being "on your own" as a writer meant. This was exciting; he could do this now; he did not need another class to do it, for a teacher could not make him do it; it was something he must do himself.

Apparently, what Charles had discovered was a new role for the self, a writer's role. This new role was opposed to his old "good student" role, for in this role he was on his own and teachers could not teach him. This new role involved behaving much as Lillian and Mark had behaved in class, facing up to certain basic problems in writing and using a small group to overcome them:

> Joy's not going to do anything much but point you in the right direction. She deals with the basic problems you'll face in any writing from a letter to a friend to a term paper. . . . You need small groups, need communication with your reader, and need to be able to see the transformation from rough to polished in others' work. I'm planning on starting a writing group with a guy in Omaha I know, that's part of a step I need to take.

Charles's small group in Joy's class had been so powerful, so clearly a model for him of what he could be doing but wasn't, that he intended to form his own group outside of school. He had, in short, developed a role for himself as writer from his experience, knew what kind of behavior this role required, and was set to try it out. The fact that this new role had little to do with school did not bother him at this point— it was an important enough role to discover that its disjunction with school roles hardly mattered:

> I'll look back on class as a turning point, the time I decided to change how I wrote, how I think, how I managed and disciplined myself.

Writing Workshops, Identity Development, and Writers' Roles

The dynamics of student responses to Joy's writing workshop are, as might be expected, qualitatively different from those of the first two classes I presented. As in the earlier classes, students' learning was clearly a function of their identity negotiations in the classroom, a function of the way they positioned themselves relative to the available roles. But unlike student responses in the earlier classes, the responses in this class have an element of conversion experience in them.

During the semester, students described themselves as changing their minds about writing, about what they might do with it in the future. Students like Bob and Charles developed new understandings of themselves as writers (Bob changing from a "capture the moment" inspired writer to a writer who recognized the importance of response and revision; Charles changing from a good "assigned topic" student writer to someone exploring a commitment to an ongoing self-sponsored writing group). Students like Gwen and Tim changed less dramatically, but still described a change (Gwen by elaborating a wider range of writing she would develop as a writer; Tim by exploring a use for writing that had frightened him in the past). In working out their stances towards the roles of this classroom, students found themselves positively altering their understanding of writing and themselves.

Obviously, something had happened in this course which was qualitatively different from what had happened in the preceding two courses. By shifting the structure of the class, Joy made it possible for students to explore writers' roles much more thoroughly and immediately than students had been able to do in the audience and Piagetian classes. Since students and teacher worked "as writers" who were developing texts according to their own agendas, they were able to apply the class's writers' roles directly to concerns outside the classroom. Consequently, the set of roles surrounding teacher-student relationships proved less important than the writers' roles operating in the classroom.

In working out their responses to presented writers' roles, individual students clarified them for themselves and often explored or adopted them as roles they would take on for the future. The workshop allowed students, in other words, to learn about writing in such a way that writing became a part of their ongoing lives. This kind of learning was not evident in the same way or degree in the classes I described in chapters 3 and 4: in those classes, it was the unusual student who made such a connection. George in the audience class and Amy in the Piagetian class were more or less unique. In the workshop class, however, students were able to focus their learning in ways which might directly influence their future selves.

The kind of changes which occurred, though, were not in any simple way programmed by the teacher—nor could they be. Instead of simply adopting the writer's role as reflective communicator which Joy modeled, each individual student clarified or changed her or his own sense of writers' roles. The process of clarification and change was influenced by the role Joy presented, but it was also influenced by the student's past, the roles the student felt already comfortable with, and a number of conflicting roles present in Joy's classroom. Any individual student's process of negotiating a particular stance amid these various influences was consequently unique, and to a degree the roles each student developed (for writers, for the self) were therefore also unique. There was no direct teacher-to-student, one-to-one correspondence between what Joy presented and what students learned.

As must now be apparent, a workshop class is set up to allow for a structured interaction among competing roles, to allow for role exploration and clarification within a reasonably secure context. A workshop allows students to learn primarily by the process of role negotiation, by working out among various examples and competing ideas what writers' roles might be and how they might operate. Instead of obscuring this negotiation under the weight of unclear or overly hierarchical teacher-student roles, a workshop allows people to explore and clarify writers' roles more or less normally: by interacting as writers with other writers, in a structured, relatively safe, but pluralistic context.

As the case studies in this chapter document, students feel that these role negotiations in workshops are beneficial. They express various kinds of conversion to writing; they articulate new understandings of their roles as writers. Workshop courses, in other words, affect students at an emotional and personal level—they feel changed by their experience. The students in this chapter all describe themselves as different, better writers as a consequence of their class.

But this feeling of change or conversion is not the only effect of writing workshops. In the next chapter, Joy Ritchie will describe changes in students' writing itself during the course of a workshop. Along with an affective change in how they feel about writing, students also change their uses of writing and their writing processes.

Because of (1) the writers' roles made available in workshop classrooms and (2) the pluralistic context that surrounds these roles, students are able to explore their writing in relation to other roles they take on in their worlds. They write in relation to their developing career roles, their family and interpersonal roles, their religious roles, and so on. They write in the presence of other students who are as diverse as the culture from which they come, so the responses they receive to their work represent the plurality of audiences of the surrounding culture. As students work out new understandings of their roles as writers, they are consequently also enriching their abilities to write professionally and personally in their pluralistic communities. As they clarify their new roles as writers, they find themselves clarifying some of their other roles as well.

6 Connecting Writers' Roles to Social Roles beyond the Classroom

Joy Ritchie

Teachers sometimes assume that students check their personal and political histories at the classroom door. In this chapter, I show how students used writers' roles to connect writing to the identity issues they were attempting to negotiate in their lives beyond the classroom— their roles as gendered selves, their religious and social identities, and the implications of economic and political issues to their immediate lives.

I argue that the writing workshop provides an effective environment for preparing students to become writers, contributing members of academic and professional communities, and effective citizens precisely because the workshop invites students to connect writing to their ongoing negotiation of roles as students, as family members, and as members of communities outside academia. In the writing workshop, students' growth as writers is inseparably intertwined with their growth as people.

I draw here on my experiences as a participant-observer working with students in a beginning writing course that Robert Brooke taught during the spring of 1986. I was struck in that class by the different responses of students and by the varied paths they followed in their growth as writers. While the class presented the same opportunities and environment for each student, they each took those possibilities and made something entirely unique of them. As I read their writing and spoke with them in extensive interviews, I began to understand that their unique responses were tied to the individual themes or agendas of their lives. The writing they did was directly implicated in the identity negotiations they were engaged in both inside and outside the writing class.

Some students, often those who were sophomores and juniors and who had chosen their major or decided on a likely career, used the workshop to articulate and clarify their identities in specific academic or professional communities. Dave, for example, was a business major who already worked in an insurance firm. His courses in the business college raised questions about the ethics of some insurance practices. He wrote two essays examining those issues. But he did not explore them from a neutral stance; he adopted the writerly role of the workshop, which urged him to connect the issues to his own experience and values and to see the problem also from various perspectives. Thus he used writing to explore his professional identity, in a sense to answer the question, "Is this the sort of person I want to become?"

Another student, Rick, whose parents were both deaf, wrote about the pros and cons of being raised by deaf parents and, in another draft, about the political debates surrounding the state school for the deaf. Both essays helped him define his relationship to his family experience; in the second essay he also claimed a role which said, "Because of my understanding of my experience as the child of deaf parents, I will be a person who can speak to important social and political questions concerning deaf people."

Other students—like Steve, who wrote about the way his school treated black athletes—adapted the writers' roles the workshop offered to reexamine their high school experiences. Still others explored roles as creative writers or journalists in order to examine family history, divorces, or marriages as the basis either for fiction or for a journalistic approach to social concerns.

The workshop class allowed students to join their lives as students-writers to the identity negotiations they were already involved in. In this chapter, I examine specifically the way three students—Brad, Becky, and Dan—connected the writers' roles the class offered to their wider emerging identities. Their responses to the class, their writing, and their interaction with the teacher and with other students illustrate the extent to which important personal issues such as gender, religion, social values, and economic class are implicated in students' development as writers.

Becky's struggles as a writer were intertwined with an exploration of her roles as a female student and as a daughter and with the struggles for authority involved in those relationships. She asks: "What have I experienced in my family? If it hasn't been all peaceful and pleasant, how do I then think about my relationship to my family?"

The central question in Brad's writing and in his personal struggles during the semester can be summed up as: "How can I be a devout, thinking Christian and also communicate persuasively my convictions to others? What does it mean when my peers challenge the validity of my convictions, and how should I respond?"

Dan's writing examined a major shift in his expectations for adult life brought on by the farm economic crisis. Though he resisted the writers' roles the workshop held out to him, he used writing to explore and articulate the conflicts he faced as he revised his view of himself as a farmer and attempted to envision a new adult life for himself in an urban setting. He attempted to find an answer to the questions: "Who am I if I'm not a farmer? What will my life be like?"

When students are confronted with new assumptions about their roles as student-writer, assumptions which simultaneously encourage them to connect their writing to important issues in their lives, the dynamics of students' responses become very complicated. As Robert has shown, students do not automatically acquiesce to the new positions the workshop makes possible. As they use those roles to serve their unique identity needs and as they engage in ongoing exploration that leads to new shifts in their perception of themselves as writers and as students, new patterns of learning emerge that cannot be reduced to easy or predictable outcomes. Among the factors likely to impinge on their work in the writing workshop are students' educational and literacy histories, their gender, family, religious, and political relationships, their relationships with peers in the collaborative environment of the workshop, and the exposure to pluralistic perspectives that occurs in such a collaborative setting.

The Teacher as Working Writer and as Authority

Previous chapters show how important teachers are in establishing a particular environment in which the negotiation of student and writer identities can take place. In this chapter, I want to focus on students and the way the writing workshop allows them to explore and restructure relationships and identities beyond the class. But teachers, past and present, became part of the scene within which students played out their own dramas in Robert's class. Teachers were particularly important because the role which Robert adopted conflicted with students' long-held assumptions about teachers and writers.

Students in Robert's class described their previous experiences in writing classrooms in ways that corroborate studies like Arthur Applebee's *Contexts for Learning to Write.* Applebee demonstrates that the chief function of writing in schools is seldom speculative or exploratory, but is usually evaluative, to test mastery of subject matter or conformity to institutional conventions. When Robert asked students during the first class to describe their previous writing, most acknowledged that they had written only in school, that writing had been on assigned topics and in traditional forms—research papers, essays, reports, and business memos. A few had been in creative writing courses, which they saw as having little use for their academic or professional careers.

Absent from their experience was writing as an act of discovery, reflection, and critical thought—writing as a genuine act of meaning making. Students also expressed no conception that writing can be a social act with consequences in people's lives beyond that of gaining a grade or certification of having mastered a set of conventions. These students generally conceived of writing as performing a task that requires one to retrieve a fixed body of information and reproduce it in a form acceptable to the teacher and institution.

Students arriving in Robert's class quickly found that he held considerably different assumptions about writing and his role as a writing teacher. As they finished describing their experience as writers on the first day of class, Robert said: "I hear you saying you've always done writing imposed on you rather than writing that comes out of your own experience and for your own purposes." Robert made clear his own different view of writing:

> My belief is that writing can be a tool to help us learn things, accomplish things for us. I want us to explore some aspects of writing, to find out things with writing.... You come up with projects that you want to do to accomplish something you want to achieve and . . . we'll work together on those . . . so they will do what you want to have accomplished.

Robert organized his class to allow writing to work in the manner he described. The class met two days a week. Tuesdays were set aside for in-class writing, initially to work through invention activities and also to practice responding to writing and, later, to engage in various strategies designed to help students reflect on and revise their writing. Thursdays were set aside for small group response. One week students met with small groups to read aloud and respond spontaneously to drafts. In the alternate week, they handed out copies of drafts on Tuesday with questions they wanted their peers and Robert to respond to in writing. Then each group met with Robert on Thursday to discuss the drafts they had read. He expected students to keep a journal in which they experimented with ideas for writing and to have a new draft or a revision each week for their group. He read and evaluated the journals twice during the semester and held conferences with students to arrive at an assessment of their work. By the end of the semester, he expected them to have completed fifteen to twenty pages of polished writing and to submit one essay for publication in the class anthology.

This class structure allowed Robert more latitude than a typical instructor has. He did not give students rules for writing or assign specific writing tasks. Instead, he established himself as working writer in the class, modeling two interconnected functions of writing: writing as exploration and writing as a rhetorical, social act. He wrote with students during invention activities, brought his evolving drafts to the class, and talked about the particular ways he and other writers work, their problems and attempts to solve them.

He invited students to join in exploring ideas they were interested in, to generate and develop topics for writing over a period of weeks, and to shape their writing according to the purpose and audience that emerged as they worked on and rethought a given piece. Rather than lecturing about writing, he frequently read his rough drafts aloud to the class and sought students' advice about how he might continue revising the piece. Using his own writing, he modeled heuristics students might use to develop ideas, to revise and reshape their writing. When he came into class one day, he said,

> I've written another draft of this letter about my sister. I thought I had it figured out, but when I got to the end I found what I had to say as a conclusion was a better idea. That's worth talking about. Writers make messes, play around with different ways of looking at their ideas. It tends to produce a lot better writing.

Robert's writing was reflective and exploratory, but at the same time he urged students: "Try to find topics you care about and do some writing which will help in your world, solve problems, and find solutions for you." Writing in his class was more than simply a performance to be evaluated. It was a means through which people could explore ideas and take action to effect change.

Robert extended his emphasis on the social function of writing by suggesting that writers need to consider the audience and purpose for their writing in order to revise it more effectively. Peer readers were an important part of the process. He modeled useful questions writers might ask their small group members, thus asserting that students were capable of providing worthwhile responses to their peers' writing, an idea that also contradicted much of students' previous experience. His own response to students' writing, as a working member of a small group and as a participant in each small group discussion on alternate weeks, was always directed by the questions students asked their group members, and it always remained nonevaluative. He encouraged students to continue writing, to attempt to find the "center" or focus for their writing by considering what they wanted to accomplish and for what audiences the writing might function. The writer's role presented to students in this class suggested that to write is to become a reflective, exploratory thinker. But it also emphasized that writers are rhetoricians, in the sense that they learn to become persuasive spokespersons on public issues.

The writerly rather than teacherly role that Robert adopted held corresponding implications for students' own positions and became a source of resistance and tension for students. Robert's stance as working writer called into question the roles they had become adept at playing in schools. During the first few classes, several students voiced their frustration: "I'm not used to this write-anything-you-want business." "I feel lost when I have the whole world to write about." "I can do pretty well, if someone tells me the direction to take." The assumptions about writing and writers that Robert modeled implied a much more responsible and autonomous role for students, a role welcomed by some and questioned by others.

In their midterm and final evaluations of the course, however, students rated it very high. They especially praised the "relaxed," "unstructured," "no pressure" atmosphere of the class, the freedom to work at their own pace and to work on projects of importance to them, and the growth they sensed in their writing. But others admitted that it had been difficult to adjust to the freedom the course offered, because they were not, in their words, "disciplined or responsible" as they should have been, and it was thus easy to "space off" the writing or attending class when other courses or activities made demands on them.

Becky: From Silence to Autonomous Voice

Writing teachers often describe learning to write as either a process of finding a "voice" or a process of taking on the conventions of a given discourse community. Becky arrived in Robert's class as a competent and successful school writer. She had mastered the requirements of school writing, but she was essentially voiceless and silent in that writing. Adrienne Rich and other feminist critics have written about the position of women students in academic institutions. In "Taking Women Students Seriously" (*On Lies, Secrets, and Silence*), Rich defines what women need from an education. In addition to a knowledge of women and their history, women students need to learn to think critically, to use their own lived experience to test assumptions, to refuse to accept what are considered givens, and to make connections that have been left unconnected (245). Rich's assessment describes generally the possibilities for redefinition and resistance that the writing workshop offered Becky. As she began to think of herself as a writer and to use writing to reexamine the social and political scene of her life, her writing allowed her to negotiate her own position in relation to two institutions which held power over her life—the family and the school. She learned that writing is more than complying with expectations of authorities and institutions, that her own experience provided a ground on which to think critically and to claim her own authority. She also learned the necessity of resisting others' definitions and, instead, of naming her own reality and thus of taking responsibility for her writing.

Becky was unprepared at first for the personal choices the workshop presented her. In high school, she had been very successful writing "informative factual" reports, which she was able to produce "the night before they were due" and for which she received "good grades," because her papers were error-free and provided tidy summaries of issues or information. In an interview, Becky told me how she had learned to identify "what teachers wanted" to please those in authority. When Robert suggested that she find issues or topics she was interested in or cared about and explore them through writing, she was confused and frustrated. In my first interview with her she explained:

> I'm having a problem because.... He says write what you want to write.... I'm used to doing assigned topics, and I've never had a class where I've had to write my own experiences. It's all been mostly research, informative, so I'm not used to putting [in] "I's" and "me's"... I don't know... it just seems like everything about me is too boring to write about.

Becky's accommodating, compliant behavior had stunted her development as a writer and as a person. As Goffman says, the total acceptance of a social role implies a kind of "selflessness." This was Becky. Submerged in her "good girl-student" role, her writing showed little evidence of a self or a "voice." She had given herself over to the norms of traditional school writing, which was "objective, impersonal, and factual" and which negated her own experience and insight. It did not allow her to engage in dialogue with authorities, neither teachers, textbooks, nor her potential readers. This is evident in the first piece she brought to class. Because she could not think of anything to write, she brought in two pages from a high school term paper on adolescent development:

> Adolescence is a part of the life cycle which is bound by puberty on one side and reaches the status of adulthood on the other.

> Adolescence, on average, includes a twelve year time span, from
> about eleven years of age to the mid-twenties. This is a period
> of "storm and stress," or more accurately seen as a period when
> an individual must move from the status of child with few rights
> and responsibilities, to the status of adult.

Becky wrote about an issue very close to her personal experience as
an adolescent, but she completely distanced herself from her subject
and wrote in a manner that denied her own authority. Like the women
Pamela Annas describes in her writing class ("Style as Politics"), Becky
needed to ground her writing in her own life experience rather than
surmount it. She needed to find her own authority and to separate
herself from total compliance with external authority.

Becky remained confused and frustrated with Robert's insistence
that she find what was important to her and be critically reflective
about her experience and her writing. But she began to do what she
thought would "satisfy what the teacher wanted," that is, to find topics
she was interested in exploring and which would interest her readers.
As she did so, her small group supported her as she took up the role
of reflective thinker and writer.

The writing of Becky's classmates provided her with models and
with a repertoire of styles and voices to imitate. Students in her small
group wrote humorously, seriously, formally, and sarcastically about
grandparents, hometowns, parents' divorces, high school experiences,
and about their complaints concerning roommates and dorm food.
Having interpreted Robert's initial response to her paper on adolescence
as critical of her writing and more accepting of their writing, she began
listening more closely to the students in her group, both for subjects
and for ways of going about writing.

As Becky began to experiment with essays about her grandfather,
her relationship with her adolescent brother, her inability to get along
with her roommates, and her family's sheep-raising enterprise, her
group's response affirmed that her ideas and experiences were interesting
and worth articulating. The group's responses consistently said, "Tell
us more about you. How did you react? What did you do next? This
is interesting, because I've never experienced this or seen it this way.
This is funny; what else did he say? Give us more details, more
incidents."

As Becky's group pushed her continually to expand and experiment
with her writing, writing became a genuine source of exploration and
reflection on her experience. Through her own writing, she began to
develop a clearer sense of herself, and she began to examine the social
roles which constructed her identity. She did not merely accept these

roles as givens with which she had to comply, but through writing, placed them in critical perspective, re-presenting her experiences to herself from different vantage points. The consequence of this critical perspective is the capacity for what Adrienne Rich, in *On Lies, Secrets, and Silences*, calls re-vision, "the act of looking back, of seeing with fresh eyes, of entering an old text from a new critical direction" ("When We Dead Awaken: Writing as Re-Vision," 35). "Re-vision" does not simply mean seeing more clearly; it also becomes the impetus for resisting old patterns and beginning to forge new ones.

I want to trace Becky's "re-vision" of her experience from the beginning of the semester through a series of drafts she worked on for the entire term. Before she abandoned the essay on adolescence in the second week of the semester, she wrote a new conclusion for it which established one of the themes that continued in her writing for the remainder of the semester:

> To improve the way we feel about ourselves we may start by learning more about ourselves and our families. Since these years are filled with hurt and conflicting feelings, we could try to work with our parents instead of against them; even though some of us would like to reject our parents and their controls. Going off to college may be a way of rejecting our parents' controls.

Becky began her exploration in a draft about her strained relationship with her younger brother, in a draft describing her grandfather, and finally in an extended exploration of her family's sheep-raising enterprise. The essay began as a simple description of how the family began raising sheep and the details of raising and showing sheep. The initial draft glorified sheep-raising as the epitome of true American family togetherness. But even in the first draft, in a sentence she intended to be humorous, she also alluded to the conflicts among family members when they worked with the sheep.

In revising the last paper six times over a three-month period, Becky tried out several different vantage points from which to view her experience. In successive drafts she wrote about sheep-raising from several perspectives: as a dispassionate journalist telling why raising sheep is a good experience for families; as an experienced sheep-raiser telling other 4-H students how to avoid the pitfalls one might encounter; as a farm kid, now college student, giving her peers from the city an entertaining, poetic, and sympathetic view of rural life; as a speech for a campus group she belonged to; and finally as a young adult reflecting on the nature of her family relationships revealed in their behavior while working with sheep. The focus of each draft remained her family, yet her writing suggested an evolving understanding of the anger and conflicts that were also part of her relationship with her parents. She moved from such statements as, "Raising sheep is an excellent family project," to "Raising sheep has advantages and disadvantages because of the problems and family conflicts involved," to finally "Parents should help their children, but they should not interfere or try to take control as my parents did."

Writing about her family allowed Becky to more honestly reflect on and reevaluate her family relationships, her stance toward parental authority, and her desire for independence. A number of feminist theorists have written about the importance of the critical perspective that women's narratives make possible for themselves and for other women. Writing allowed Becky finally to be honest about her anger and to recognize the importance of her family in her life without masking the realities of her relationship with them.

In an interview at the end of the semester, she described the understanding she had gained from writing and revising that essay:

> It gave me a chance to write about myself and I'm not used to that. . . . I could dig deeper into how I felt about things. . . . I learned . . . I don't know . . . I learned I had some real commitments and some strong opinions. It started out as something I took for granted . . . with some negative feelings about my family raising sheep, and I know I would do things different from my parents, but . . . it wasn't all bad, I realize that it probably brought us together. It was a fairly positive thing, and I guess . . . I see the whole experience differently.

Becky connected the role of writer as reflective thinker with her need to understand her family and to express the resentment she held toward her parents' attempts to exert control over her. She also connected it to her need to redefine her compliant position toward the authority of the teacher.

Henry Giroux as well as feminist critics like Adrienne Rich and Judith Fetterley have noted the importance of resistance, the need of people on the margins to refuse to assent to definitions of self and reality which dominant institutions seek to impose on them. The workshop would seem to be the ideal place for a student like Becky to reclaim her own experience and redefine her important social relationships. But doing so in her case also meant reexamining the assumptions she had held about teachers and her relationship with them. Becky's ability to resist accommodation to prescribed roles was played out in tangible terms in her response to Robert. As she began to reshape those writers' roles to her own purposes, she also inevitably resisted some of Robert's suggestions about her writing, using this resistance as a step toward maintaining control over her writing and her emerging definition of her experience.

At the beginning of the class, Becky responded to Robert as she had to previous teachers. He was the authority figure from whom she would seek approval. She set about trying to figure out the rules the instructor expected her to follow so that she could comply and win his approving evaluation. But Robert did not judge the writing she brought to the small group. He suggested instead that she keep writing, and he provided other suggestions in the form of options: "You could decide to go this direction with the paper, or you could scrap that idea you began with and go with the idea you've begun talking about here at the end . . . depending on what you want to accomplish and who your audience might be."

This confused and frustrated Becky, and she watched closely to determine what sort of judgment lay beneath his response:

> I'm trying to figure out what he wants. . . . But he always says, "Well, what do you want to know?" And he'll sit there until we let him know, and once you let him know, he starts to ask you who the audience might be. . . . Everyone else he likes . . . they may have to add a little bit, but he tells *me* to forget about the beginning or work from the ending . . . I don't think mine's any worse than anybody else's, but it seems that he has the most comments for mine.

In her previous experience she received immediate approval for her writing, and now there was no immediate possibility of determining whether she had succeeded or not.

Becky's need for approval was complicated by conditions outside the class, especially pressure she felt from her family. She was a second-semester freshman, and she felt she had to decide quickly on a major. Since she was considering majoring in journalism or English, it was imperative that she get a clear sense of whether she was "good enough," because her parents could not afford for her to "waste time" taking a lot of classes to try out another major. She was looking for an answer from her professor, but it was not forthcoming.

During the first half of the semester, Robert's written and oral responses continued to encourage her to write and revise, to refine for herself the audience and purpose for writing each piece. Near the end of the semester in response to Becky's question, "Am I done with this?" he attempted to show her more directly how to make her essay more coherent, logical, and polished. But Becky now resisted his advice:

> Robert said, "I liked from the second page on a lot . . . as you talk about your family . . . but I found myself again surprised

... getting switched into that, because I thought it was going to be about the advantages of raising sheep, and it's not."

"Yes it is," replied Becky. "But *you're* not reading it right."

"Let me show you why I'm not seeing it. (The instructor reads, pointing to places in the text where his focus is shifted from the advantages and disadvantages to her discussion of family dynamics.) You could try adding a sentence that goes something like this ... at the beginning to show how the pieces all fit together."

"Well, I'll think about it." Becky sighed.

Becky resisted his suggestions, saying that she liked it the way it was and that *he* was confused. But she also resisted because to adopt his suggestions, to impose more coherence, to make her writing more "reader-based" would result in a conceptualization of her experience according to another person's view, according to the view of an authority figure. And it would force her to return to the compliant "good girl" stance she was just beginning to shed. She resisted creating tidy, "reader-based" prose when it implied giving up ownership of that text and imposing traditional forms in place of her own. At the beginning of the semester Becky wanted the instructor to be the authority figure who would evaluate her writing and tell her she was "good enough," but by the end, despite her continued need for approval and her pragmatic need to be finished with the paper, she resisted his attempt to help organize and impose closure on her text.

Becky's need as a developing writer to claim control over her own language and experience was in conflict here with the need to produce polished academic prose by the end of the semester. As her sense of ownership over her writing grew, she was unwilling to retreat to her earlier strategies of merely satisfying the demands of the teacher-authority. She realized she had choices to make, and she determined to work out the problems for herself. This is no small step for a young woman in a male-dominated academic institution. It may be an exaggeration to view Becky's resistance to Robert in such dramatic terms, but perhaps it is impossible to exaggerate the importance of women students assuming power to name their own reality and thus to control their own lives.

When I asked Becky to reflect on the course at the end of the semester, she not only spoke about the new perspectives writing had given her on her social and family relationships, she also enumerated ways that her writing had changed and improved in style and organization, many of which she attributed to Robert's class, and she also described how her process of writing had changed. Although she speaks with some ambiguity about her confidence in her writing, she speaks, I believe, with a clearer understanding of herself as writer and student, a more autonomous and powerful student and writer than she had been before:

> I used to make my rough draft close to the final one. Now I build it more. He helped us a lot with rewriting and now I do more of that. . . . Even in theater and sociology, I've started to add more details and descriptions. . . . I dig into things more now. . . . So far I'm getting A's there. I used to think I was a decent writer, now sometimes I'm not so sure. . . . It takes a lot of time and concentration. It got me really aggravated at times. It used to be a lot easier. I've always liked to write, but now I really know that it's not good enough when I just write it the night before. Really writing takes much more. I get confused and frustrated, thinking of all the choices to make, what to put in and where, but I keep trying . . . and I like Robert, but he also makes me mad sometimes with his suggestions. He always could see different ways the paper might go, but I could usually work it out, so I kept writing. I know it just takes more time to improve.

Becky took on the writerly role and joined that role to the personal and social issues that were most pressing in her life. In the process, she began to piece together a new understanding of her roles within her family and academic community and her anticipated roles as an adult. This was a process, then, of helping her develop beyond the student role to the more complex family and professional roles she will assume. In those roles she will be less likely now to parrot uncritically the ideas of some authority or to accommodate her behavior to the demands of others in order to gain their approval.

Furthermore, the writing workshop with its student-centered environment allowed Becky to develop autonomy within a context that was not only supportive but collaborative. She did not learn a writerly role that was individualistic or solitary, any more than she learned to overaccommodate to some academic discourse community. Rather, as Becky moves through her degree program in English and journalism and then into either the academic or professional world, she promises to be a person who can use writing to understand herself and her experiences and to critically reexamine the world around her. And she will also understand the value of working cooperatively with others.

Brad: From Authoritarian to Dialogic Stance

Brad used the writer-student roles made available in the writing workshop to serve very different themes in his identity development. He immediately adapted his desire to be a persuasive spokesman for his religious community to Robert's assertion that writing can serve to address important issues and create change. Brad felt compelled to convince others of the validity of his Catholic religious beliefs and to persuade people to adopt his religious and moral philosophy. In the collaborative setting of the writing workshop, he found that this "missionary" role and the manner he assumed in his attempts to communicate were unacceptable to many of his fellow students. Thus his writing and interaction in the writing class created a conflict which forced him to redefine his relationship to his religious beliefs and to his peers.

Like the other students, Brad had difficulty at first figuring out what kind of writing Robert wanted them to do, but he listened closely to the writing Robert read during the first few classes, writing that Robert suggested students use to "explore their world and to help them solve problems." Brad did not understand that writing can serve as reflection and exploration, but he did understand "writing about problems and solutions." As he noted the reactions others had to Robert's writing, Brad attributed to it the qualities he hoped to achieve in his own writing—"logic," "forcefulness," "persuasiveness." But he did not realize the scope of Robert's assumptions about writing, nor could he see that changing writing entailed more than changing an empty shell and taking on another one. He did not see that changing his writing would also change him.

Brad's previous experiences with writing and religious education were important influences on his underlying understanding of the processes by which people arrive at and communicate knowledge and meaning. He came to the class from a traditional high school program which he described as having emphasized the careful construction of "logical essays" on topics supplied by the teacher. Students developed essays with thesis statements and supporting facts, and these essays were evaluated according to their correspondence to formal requirements established by the teacher. Brad's definition of writing went something like this: The writer makes an assertion of some stance on an issue, then proceeds to support that assertion with "facts" or "statistics" that he believes will prove a point. His writing experience in school had emphasized exclusive attention to form and message.

For Brad, writing had little to do with the writer's critical examination and interpretation of such "facts" based on his own experience or knowledge. Nor did his previous writing instruction suggest that part of the task writers face is exploring the complexities of issues and considering the multiple perspectives an issue might encompass, the various viewpoints one's readers might hold, or the necessity of considering the rhetorical strategies that might make for the most effective presentation of ideas. Brad's earlier instruction had given him little experience using writing as a means of speculation and investigation or practice at considering the rhetorical context in which a particular piece of writing might function. In addition, his writing in school had promoted dualistic and reductionist notions of "fact," "truth," and "knowledge."

These notions were reinforced by Brad's religious instruction. In conversations with me and members of his small group, he indicated that he spent a good bit of time in activities at his church's campus center and that he had been on a retreat with other students who were considering going to seminary. The reading, writing, and speaking he valued in his religious community (some of which he quoted in his essays) also emphasized the dualistic thinking and prescriptive rhetorical conventions he had become accustomed to in school. Speculative, multiple, or ambiguous perspectives and potentially divergent values and beliefs among one's audience had little place in his conception of writing. Furthermore, the idea that writers examine and interpret their experience, that they discover and construct knowledge in the process of writing and reading, and that they might actually engage in dialogue with readers was not a part of Brad's experience. Instead, one wrote either to satisfy the requirements of the educational institution or to dictate to others what to believe.

While Becky at the beginning of the course felt her task was to figure out and fulfill the demands of the teacher, Brad interpreted Robert's goals so that they matched his own. He wanted to learn to write persuasively because that was part of the role a priest or missionary took on. But as he undertook his own writing, it became apparent that he could not be persuasive without changing the nature of his writing, his thinking, and his relationship with his readers—changes that would result in a transformation of the position he held in class with his peers and in his religious community.

The social relationships made possible in the writing workshop provided the context in which Brad could grow as a writer and, in the process, reassess his social relationships with peers and church. These changes occurred, first, because the writing workshop provided a supportive and nonevaluative environment. Consequently, Brad was able to see Robert as a model of a writer's behavior and as a supportive ally in his attempts to write. Second, the writing workshop provided Brad, for the first time, with an immediate audience of his peers so that he was able to see the impact his writing had on readers who were not teachers. Third, the writer-reader roles other students constructed in this class created alternatives to the role Brad had always assumed students ought to play. The dynamic of the writing workshop worked upon the educational, religious, and intellectual history he brought to class to become a catalyst for change in his thinking and writing.

In the first week of class, Brad set out to produce writing that worked as successfully as Robert's had. But because of the dogmatic stance he assumed on controversial topics, his writing was not well received. The first essay he brought to class was titled "The Working Mother." In it he cited statistics about the increasing numbers of women who are working, and he argued that they are not working out of economic necessity, but because of the women's movement. In addition he said that the large number of working mothers is destructive to "traditional family values."

Brad distributed his essay to his group with this note: "This is written from a Christian viewpoint. Do you agree that children more and more often now grow up in families where both parents work? Do you see the logic of this paper?" Brad had not shed his earlier assumptions that there are always clear, right answers to problems revealed by "facts" and that one either agrees or disagrees. (In this case to agree meant "you are a logical person like me.") The essay evoked a strong negative reaction from the members of his small group. One young woman argued with him and wrote these vehement notes on a copy of his paper, then returned it to him:

> I don't agree . . . it is not traditional in all cultures . . . why not both parents caring for children? . . . Seventy-five percent of work- ing women *must* work whether they want to or not. . . . You try to justify yourself by saying you are a traditionalist. You assume tradition is the proper way . . . you are too set in your ways. If you would only take time to stop or listen to other people's viewpoints.

This response was a negative reaction not simply to Brad's paper, but to the identity he assumed as a writer of this piece, a dogmatic and prescriptive persona his peers disliked. His peer readers were also unwilling to become the sort of silenced, bullied, uncritical audience his paper invoked. His strategies might work in sermons or to satisfy English teachers, but they would not work with an audience of his peers.

By the third week of the course, it became clear to Brad that there was more than "logic" and "forcefulness" behind the success of Robert's writing. In his class, Robert was suggesting that students write to explore issues and experiences to which their very identity was tied. In addition, he was suggesting that if writing is to help solve problems or create awareness among readers, writers must look at their writing from a variety of perspectives in order to revise for the most effective presentation of ideas.

Although Robert said he was nervous about overemphasizing audience, he tried to help students find ways to take into account the knowledge, values, and beliefs of their readers. He brought this to students' attention in several ways. First he asked students to work frequently in small groups to discuss ideas about which they were writing so that they could see tangibly how their ideas affected potential readers. Second, he engaged students in writing and group strategies to help them explore their purpose and audience for a given piece and to examine the perspectives those readers might have on a particular topic.

On one occasion Robert talked explicitly about audience:

> Anytime I write, I'm after the mind of the reader. Everyone has a different model of the world they live in. There are several ways we can change that view of the world. . . . When we're working with a piece of writing, we need to ask ourselves what types of changes we're trying to promote. . . . We also need to consider our authority and position with respect to the audience we're addressing. . . . What role do we assume? How do we go about establishing our authority, and how do we take into consideration their position?

Robert's words here had an important impact on Brad, who repeated them almost verbatim to me in an interview a few days later. Robert also used his own writing to illustrate how he might revise, given a particular set of readers. Thus he allowed Brad to begin to see how as a writer he might shift from the almost exclusive focus on text structure and dogmatic message to a concern for communicating his message effectively to readers whose values and ideas were different from his own, readers who might even question authority.

Brad's next paper was once again an attempt to articulate his religious beliefs, but to do so in a manner that would be less offensive to his response group. He described it as "presenting a series of logically related facts that are vital to the validity of a church. . . . I want to point out that there is one truth." The resulting draft was a confused blend of dualistic thinking and dogmatic style with writing that attempted to consider more sensitively his peer audience:

> There are many people and churches that claim to be legitimate and true churches. . . . How can so many churches make this claim? . . . This was not always the case. Only in the last four hundred years has this been the case. But to discuss this one must first discuss truth. Webster's dictionary defines truth as the "real

state of things," and "facts." Truth must be singular... and it follows that anything else is an untruth or a lie.

Brad tried to mitigate the dogmatic tone and the negative effect on his readers by attempting to trace the history of the church in a casual, "humorous" tone:

> Then comes along good 'ole Henry IV, with his eight wives. He decides he wants to marry his servant girl, but the Pope re-fuses... so what does he do? But of course—start another Church.... He totally breaks off from the Church which has contained the body of truth for fifteen hundred years. This was definitely not logical, but very emotional.... My, my with all that truth around you'd think the world would be better.

Although this is a very clumsy attempt at humor, Brad had begun to experiment with ways to make his ideas more palatable to a real audience of his peers. He also recognized that this attempt did not work. He made copies, but withheld them when the time came to pass them out. So he merely read the draft aloud to his group, prefacing his reading with two questions: "Does this sound comical to you?" and "Can you follow the logic of the paper?" He also acknowledged that the draft "presented little churches looking like fools."

The group's response was polite and attentive, but they refused to make any comments, until finally the student who had argued with him about the earlier essay could not contain herself. She said that she did not think the paper was humorous and that it offended her because it seemed to attack her religious beliefs. When Robert asked Brad explicitly who he thought might be his audience, Brad said he supposed he could write for members of his religious group who might find it comical. Brad found himself isolated from other students in the class. The dogmatic, missionary, zealot role he assumed in his writing was ineffective.

By midterm Brad recognized that his small group had ceased to function as a viable audience because they were too alienated by his earlier writing. Their negative response arose from the controversial subjects he chose to write about, the dogmatic tone of his writing, and the passive role he projected for them. But in a broader sense they rejected Brad's writing because it violated the norms for writerly behavior the group had created during the first several weeks of the semester. These were norms they had constructed from their interpre-tation of the writing which Robert modeled in class, from listening to and reading their own writing, and from previous experiences in this class and others. People in Brad's group wrote about families, home-towns, sports, coaches, and roommates and their exploits with friends.

They wrote to reflect on their own experiences, a function much removed from Brad's purposes for writing, because they assumed writing should explore personal experiences, or at least the writer should illustrate ideas with personal examples. It should be lively, entertaining, detailed, and it should "fit" or "flow" together instead of rambling or sounding unduly theoretical. And writing should not pursue controversial subjects in a way that might offend other students. These implied standards set Brad in direct conflict with his group. When he noted the conflict between himself and the group in an interview at midterm, he was defensive and blamed the other students:

> I found out that people shouldn't write in class about politics or religion. As soon as I mention Protestantism in my papers they go on the defensive. I guess I'm attacking the personal values of some people. . . . I feel like . . . I might as well talk to a wall. I wish they would think more deeply. I'm trying to write logical arguments, but most of their papers and reactions are purely emotional and . . . shallow topics.

Brad gave copies of drafts to his group only occasionally for the rest of the semester, but he was almost always present to read drafts aloud. Although from Robert's and my perspective his group seemed dysfunctional for Brad (so dysfunctional that Robert joined that group as a permanent member), the group's response had been invaluable to Brad. They modeled for him a different role for student writers and readers than he had seen before. They wrote to reflect on experiences such as the effects an automobile accident has in a small town and to explore particular points concerning treatment of athletes by coaches. They encouraged and supported each other with suggestions, sometimes challenging each other's perspective with questions, but never challenging one another antagonistically as they did Brad.

In general, the members of Brad's group were curious about the varied perspectives their peers brought to the class. But Brad's critical, defensive tone was unacceptable to his peers. His fellow students provided a mirror in which he could see how the "missionary, dissenter role" he was experimenting with played out in a group which represented multiple perspectives and values. The workshop provided a response Brad needed in order to explore the identity he was considering beyond the classroom. It helped him figure out what sort of stance he would take to the marginal role he found himself in.

Students' response did not lead to Brad's automatic compliance with the behavior and values the group held out for him. He still felt strongly compelled to improve his ability to write persuasively, but he would not become the kind of person whose writing they would accept.

Consequently, he no longer used them as a sounding board, but his group did continue to function as an "imagined" internalized audience, intractable and shallow as he believed they were, for his last and most lengthy paper. Although he continued participating in the group, if only in a perfunctory way, he felt himself supported in this resistance by Robert, as he indicated in an interview:

> But Robert sort of agrees with a lot of stuff I say, but he doesn't show it. . . . He's in my group now, and his writing is so much better that it really helps other people pick up on that. I believe he's right . . . that writing is a tool to get a message or thought across and he's good at that.

While the group obviously rejected Brad's ideas, Robert maintained his nonevaluative stance, and Brad, unlike Becky, interpreted that as support for his own perspective. A traditional, evaluative teacher response might have indicated to Brad how misguided, ill-conceived, and insulting his writing was, forcing Brad either to abandon topics he cared about or to "domesticate" his voice to the demands of his audience. Instead, Robert continued to respond by pointing out places where he could not follow Brad's line of thought in the essay on working mothers or by showing him where he might need to supply a great deal more evidence or might need to "slow down" and thoroughly develop the history of the church and his own thinking about it. He even told Brad, "As a reader I feel more attacked than convinced by the really quick survey you do here."

As a working writer in the class, Robert continued to pose questions about his own writing which provided questions Brad might in turn ask of his own writing. All of Robert's questions suggested that writers need to remain open to multiple perspectives and to think of their writing as a dialogue between themselves and their readers rather than as a diatribe. "How am I addressing my readers? What do my readers already think, feel, or know about this subject?" Robert tried, then, to provide a supportive environment in which Brad could continue to accomplish his own purposes for writing, one which would also supply him with new strategies and perspectives for communicating more effectively and thinking more broadly. When I asked Robert about Brad in an interview at midterm, he said:

> I don't know . . . I think increasingly he knows . . . watching him, his behavior with the group, he's beginning to see that it's not working, but it's so important to him, and he's just not making the connection yet. I hope the writing itself will change that. . . . He is talking about audience, at least he asked the question of his group, and yesterday that allowed me to point out a place or two

> where he could acknowledge the variety of perspectives on that . . .
> but I realize that's a very sneaky thing to do, because as soon as
> he starts acknowledging the variety of perspectives, it will explode
> on him and the simple case will no longer be simple. . . . So I'm
> hoping with time and . . . continuing the writing, continuing to
> see the response, the writing will get him to recognize the com-
> plexity of the issues.

Robert's stance allowed Brad to continue to experiment with his
writing. And by midterm Brad had found another topic he wanted to
address, but this time he went about it in a much more exploratory
mode, though he started from the same dogmatic position he had
assumed before. He began reading about the life of Margaret Sanger
in order to attack her efforts to promote family planning and organize
Planned Parenthood. What began as a diatribe eventually grew, over a
period of six weeks, into a fifteen-page essay his group might have
found acceptable. Brad was encouraged along by Robert's responses:

> Will your readers hold the same negative view of Margaret Sanger
> as you? Your tone assumes they are already on your side when
> you suggest that abortion is bad, pre-marital sex is bad, and
> Planned Parenthood is bad. Some readers will turn you off, picking
> up on your bias before they see your information. . . . Aren't there
> conflicting points of view, even from other authorities, you need
> to acknowledge here? . . . You don't describe the source of the
> evidence so that your readers can weigh its reliability. . . . Your
> case will be stronger and easier for your reader to follow if you
> explain your statistics more clearly and document your evidence.

In my midterm interview, Brad acknowledged that his perspective
on his writing and on readers had shifted considerably:

> I realize that I'm writing it still as a Catholic issue, and I don't
> want it to be just a Catholic issue. . . . I had never thought about
> my position, the role I was portraying in my writing and how
> readers might see my role or authority. That gave me ideas for
> the paper I'm working on. I'll have to establish credibility so
> they'll listen to me, otherwise I'll just seem like a freshman in
> college.

In successive drafts of this paper, Brad can be seen struggling to
reconcile his religious beliefs with the necessity of writing effectively,
taking into account multiple perspectives and recognizing the complexity of the issues he was writing about. His attempt to consider a
wider perspective and the resulting dialogic tone of his writing can be
seen in the introduction to his last draft of the paper:

> Planned Parenthood today is a very large and powerful orga-
> nization. More and more young people today are influenced by

it than ever before. Perhaps such an influential organization should be understood more by those who are affected by it, namely the young and the parents of the young. One can find opinions all the way from Planned Parenthood as a leader in reproductive health to being an organization that ruins the lives and thoughts of young women every year. Perhaps such an organization should be given some thought.

Although he had not changed his own beliefs, he had begun to think about the issues as more complicated and his audience as more critical and reflective. He also had learned that one can remain in a marginal or dissenter role and work within that role, but he learned to do so more effectively and thus be a better change agent. These phrases from his final draft demonstrate some of the changes in his writing:

> All these statistics cannot conclusively prove that Planned Parenthood's program is not working. Other factors must be taken into account. . . . These may be extreme examples, but they may indicate the kind of claim Planned Parenthood makes. . . . Planned Parenthood began with a program of social progress and relief for the poor. . . . Now instead of concentrating on the side effects of the problem, they should once again concentrate on the root of the problem.

Brad's writing at the end of the semester projects a much different voice and identity than his earlier writing. He is no longer the zealot, hostile or condescending to his readers. He is a more thoughtful, careful writer who takes into account the ambiguities of issues and the plural perspectives of his readers.

In our final interview, Brad articulated a more mature sense of the way writing can be used to explore a subject, and he was beginning to see more clearly the limitations of his own writing as communication to a pluralistic audience:

> This class has given me time to write on some things I wanted to work on. . . . See, what I've learned from this class, is to be a good writer you have to have something that interests other people, and even though you have interesting facts, if you can't present it in a way that helps other people, it's not effective. . . . I've re-written this paper several times, and I just re-read it and can see more I need to do before Monday. . . . You have to be very careful about being a writer so that you don't end up writing about yourself and for yourself and it doesn't apply to anyone else. . . . I'd like to keep writing. I think I can get even better.

Brad has not changed his beliefs. He has not been transformed to the tolerant, liberal humanist his professors might have liked him to become or to the easygoing, fun-loving, live-and-let-live student his peers might have liked a great deal more. Though he resisted those roles, he engaged the role of reflective thinker and persuasive rhetorician to such an extent that his writing and thinking, as we see them here, are vastly changed. Through writing he has acquired a perspective that would make it difficult to think so reductively again.

Brad was able to join what is traditionally conceived as purely academic work to the most crucial work of his life at this time—negotiating his beliefs and values, his place in his religious community, his career, and his relationship to peers. The development in Brad's thinking and writing during the semester suggests that, like Becky, he would be much more prepared to work in a complex, pluralistic social context where many values and perspectives are at play, an environment very unlike the more authoritarian academic and religious contexts that had previously governed his conception of himself as student, writer, and citizen.

With Brad and Becky we see how a complicated web of factors within the writing workshop and from students' personal lives join together to help them form different patterns of identity negotiation, each unique to the student's own history. Although some of their writing would still have seemed unpolished to some readers, Brad and Becky represent a group of students for whom Robert's class provided an opportunity for emotional and intellectual growth. They had extended writers' roles the class offered them until they encompassed their social identity negotiations outside the class. In the process, Brad and Becky also fulfilled the requirements of the course and, as Becky indicated, found support for writing in other academic areas.

Dan: Accepting the Role of Writer, but Rejecting English Class

Some students were less successful than Becky and Brad in the writing workshop. Dan was one of them. His attendance was sporadic, he failed to bring writing to small groups or brought only very rough fragments, and he did not engage in serious revision of drafts. Students like Dan were less likely to keep appointments with me for interviews and were frequently absent or did not make copies of their drafts. But because Dan was in my small group, I did get copies of his writing, heard him read some of his drafts aloud, and interviewed him twice during the semester. From his behavior and from my conversations with him, it initially appeared that he had been unable to connect the roles of the writing workshop with his role in the wider social community. But as I looked more closely at the fragments of writing he brought to class, and looked at them in relation to information about his life, I found that while overtly he resisted writing, to at least a small degree, he adapted Robert's definition of a writer's identity in order to explore a crucial question that had recently become the central focus of his life. Still, the interference of other factors in his life was so great that he could not fulfill the requirements of the course.

Dan's attitude about English classes was one problem that kept him from finding the workshop a conducive place to learn. He had decided quite definitely somewhere in his education that English was antithetical to his very nature:

> I've never been much into English. It's always sorta hard for me to write stuff. . . . I can't get time to do it. . . . If I can sit down and write something real fast I can do better. I'd rather do two pages rather than five or six. . . . See, when I first came down here, I thought I'd get into ag communication because I liked using a camera, I'd been involved in 4-H, had pictures sent away. . . . I was really into that, but I guess it's English that kept me away from it. . . . It's always been my hardest class, always dreaded it. . . . It's just . . . English has always been my downfall.

Although Dan wrote as well as many other students in the class, his belief that he was not the sort of person who "did English" was unshakable. He could not make himself sit down to write, and when he did write he did not feel that his work was worth reading. Because English was his "downfall," he even abandoned pursuing a career where he seemed to have some talent and interest. Thus he resisted joining the English class. It's "just not my thing," he said several times. He brought writing to his small group from time to time, but except for one piece, he seldom continued with an initial draft.

Other factors were involved in Dan's behavior. The economic crisis affecting farmers in Nebraska had placed him in the middle of a broad renegotiation of what he planned to do in college and during the rest of his life. He came from a farming-ranching area which had been one of the most severely affected by the farm crisis. His family had always lived on the farm, and it had been traditional for extended families to gain their livelihood working together on one piece of land. Dan came to the university planning to get a degree in agriculture and, like his older brother, planned to return to the farm after graduation. But when he went home after the first semester, his father told him that the farm could not support his brother and his parents, much less another member of the family. Thus Dan was in the midst of a major repositioning of his personal and social identity. He described his difficulties in an interview at midterm:

> That really hurt more than about anything because when my brother went to college . . . you know he didn't take college serious because he knew he was going back to farm, but it's different now . . . it can't be for me. I guess my dad's going to retire this year and he's going to take over the operation. But they're having a tough time, and he's seen what my sister's doing. She works for the soybean association and she's making about double. . . . I was going to major in ag too, but my dad thinks I should get into accounting or math or something. . . . I was going to work on beef judging this summer, but I decided I'd better do something else. So I'm looking for a job, and it's tough for me to look for jobs because you know they say, "What's your work experience?" And I say, "farming," and that's all. I can't imagine selling shoes or something. . . . I think it will be hard to be inside all the time, all summer. . . . But I moved off East campus this semester cause being there is like being on the farm sort of. It's hard . . . like breaking up with someone, I guess.

Despite his resistance to the entire idea of English and writing classes, Dan began to use writing to explore new social roles.

The first freewriting he brought to class was an attempt to outline the causes of the farm economic crisis. The essay attempted to place blame, but it shifted between blaming the bankers and the farmers themselves. Dan read the essay to his small group, and they responded by trying to help him clarify the argument he was making and to find ways to expand and organize this very complex topic. He abandoned the draft and commented at the end of the semester that he had gone back to it once or twice, but he just could not handle that topic. It was too technical and impossible to deal with.

His second draft was inspired by a group member who wrote about her family's attempts to decide what to do with her grandmother, who had Alzheimer's disease. Dan's fragmentary one-page draft told about two elderly people who lived alone in the small town near his family's farm and how dedicated their son, his neighbor, was in attending to them every day. He said, "I think this is a better way to treat old people than putting them in homes. There's a nursing home over in Ainsworth, but from what I hear . . . my girlfriend worked there one summer, it's not a very good place. . . . In small towns people stick together and help each other better."

This was the beginning of a series of partial drafts which Dan described as "comparing different lifestyles." He compared farm life to city life, student life on the agricultural campus and on city campus, where he had moved since he changed his major. His writing poked fun at the "polyester, denim and cowboy boots" on the ag campus and at "the preppy, sockless" look on city campus. With an anthropologist's eye he observed the differences in tastes ("beer vs. vodka" and "pick-ups vs. TransAms") on the two campuses. He also noted the more "unfriendly and distant" treatment he encountered on the city campus. Dan's writing then was allowing him to understand the transition he was engaged in. In an effort to prepare himself for an alien-seeming lifestyle, he analyzed and attempted to understand the culture he was leaving behind as a farmer and the one he was attempting to enter as a city person.

Dan completed only one piece of writing during the semester, a draft he worked with off and on, because, he said, "I guess I'm addicted to this issue." He said he began writing it because an article in the student newspaper about gun control made him angry. Since one of Robert's in-class invention exercises asked students to find something that made them angry and write about it, he had pursued this topic. He began arguing that "gun-control is a bad idea, because on the farm you know we always have guns and nobody gets hurt . . . we hunt all the time." But as he continued to work on this idea, he also read a magazine article and watched a talk-show with a spokesperson for handgun control. In his final draft he had switched his opinion to one arguing for gun control:

> Handguns are not needed, they are becoming more harmful everyday. . . . The saying goes: "That was then, this is now," and the adage fits America's present situation perfectly. Then, in the old days, America needed guns, now we don't. . . . Handguns should become as extict [*sic*] as the horse and buggy and the family farm.

Dan's changing position on this issue almost seems to parallel the very transition of social roles he was engaged in. His writing in this essay, a last-ditch effort to produce enough polished writing to salvage his grade for the semester, demonstrates that despite his overt rejection of English classes, the open possibilities in the writing workshop provided a space within which he could connect writing to his personal identity negotiation.

Although it is hard to say exactly what influenced Dan's choices about his attendance and general behavior with respect to Robert's class, he is like many students who, as they begin college, are engaging in a crucial process of identity negotiation. For students like Becky, taking up the role of writer-as-explorer allows them to discover and become more consciously reflective about issues surrounding their evolving selfhood. For others like Dan and Brad, those issues may already be near the surface, calling out for utterance and examination when the environment for writing becomes conducive to such reflection.

Connecting Writing with Learning outside the Classroom

At the beginning of this chapter I claimed that writing workshops provide the preparation students need to become writers and also to become more reflective people in their families and communities. I make that claim because of the kind of environment the workshop class makes possible and the definitions of writing and writers' roles it promotes. Those roles allow students to integrate writing with the most crucial issues of their developing identities, to be exposed to and examine multiple perspectives, which allow for further dialogue and redefinition of selfhood.

Lev Vygotsky (*Thought and Language*) says that teaching interacts with development and changes it. In the writing workshop, writing interacts with identity development and both writing and identity are likely to change. As Brad's and Becky's writing changed, their vocabulary for talking about writing and about their relationships with people also changed. Brad no longer talked about writing in terms of "force," "logic," and "persuasiveness." He talked about it in terms of responsiveness and dialogue. Becky no longer talked about pleasing the teacher, but about self-understanding, reexamination, and active decision making. In these students' writing and their talk about writing we can see them taking on new ways of writing, but also new ways of thinking about themselves, their social relationships and values.

The writing workshop approximates a microcosm of the pluralistic society in which students live. It is not a neutral environment. The writer's roles it makes availablefor students arise out of a very clear set of values. The workshop classroom values personal experience and self-reflection, tolerance and consideration for plural perspectives, dialogue, responsibility, and commitment to action. If students become apprentice writers in those roles, they are likely to leave the workshop better able to carry those roles into their lives as members of families and communities.

7 Writing Instruction and Writers' Roles

I began this book with the story of a shift in my teaching, a shift from sequence of assignment courses to workshop courses. In the past four years, I have been trying to understand why this shift to writing workshops produced such powerful educational experiences. I have also been trying to understand what kinds of learning principles underlie these courses. And I have been speculating about the consequences of this shift for the general purposes of writing instruction in our culture.

The case studies in this book present the classroom experiences and theories with which I have been addressing these questions. By looking at a range of classrooms from an identity negotiations perspective, I have shown (1) that learning is dependent on identity negotiations, on individuals' attempts to work out their social place in and beyond the classroom, (2) that learning to write depends on the identification and exploration of writers' roles for the self, roles which need to be broader than the limited examinee-to-examiner traditional school roles, and (3) that writing workshops are able to help students develop such writers' roles, leading to changes in self-conception and writing behavior. I have argued that learning to write really means more than just learning specific content, organizational and grammatical rules, rhetorical concepts, or writing processes—it means coming to attach to the self a set of writers' roles, negotiating an understanding of the self as someone who uses writing for personally and socially important purposes.

Such development of writers' roles has important consequences for writing instruction generally. In my teaching and thinking in the last four years, I have come to believe that the possibilities for role development in workshops can help clarify our educational mission as writing teachers. Students leave writing workshops better able to act critically in the roles they take on in their wider culture, better able to use writing to reflect on and participate in their culture's important debates. Writing workshops, therefore, may be an example to other educators of a way to promote active citizens, a way education might encourage fuller participation in our pluralistic democracy. In a time when education often works against these goals—knowingly or un-

140

knowingly—such an example can provide an important mission for teaching.

Despite Dewey's attempts to develop an active, engaged schooling, we currently have schools which are almost incompatible with or resistant to civic participation. As Frank Smith has argued (*Insult to Intelligence*), most schools are now organized according to bureaucratic principles of hierarchical authority, accountability, standardization, and testability. The result of these principles has been the kind of student-as-examinee roles I have described as interfering with real learning. When students take on these roles in schools, they become the exact opposite of participating citizens: instead of vigilant, tolerant, self-sufficient protectors of rights and freedoms, they become isolated, competitive, and authority-dependent. In a book documenting the parallel development of schools, prisons, and police forces in history (*Discipline and Punish*), Michel Foucault even argues that the unrecognized purpose for the hierarchical, normalizing, examining structure of schools is to help produce a docile populace, a populace which internalizes so well the principles of competition, authority, and isolation that they cannot imagine the possibility of opposition to dominant social forces.

In contrast to such bureaucratic classrooms, writing workshops can offer a model of participatory interaction. By allowing students to develop their own agendas for writing within a complex social setting, by encouraging tolerance and reflection concerning views different from one's own, and by providing opportunities to explore writers' roles which function outside as well as inside the classroom, writing workshops can provide a microcosm of what participatory interaction might be. It is, after all, within the complex pluralism of our ever-widening culture that writers' roles need to function. The roles we teachers make available to our students can either help them participate more fully in this widening culture or limit that participation in describable ways.

To promote incorporation of writers' roles, though, is a huge and demanding charge, given the complexity of both identity negotiation and the school context. In a context as complex as that of the classroom, the roles a teacher designs and presents are only one set of roles among others, and each student's identity negotiation will occur in the context of all the roles he or she perceives. Teachers, thus, can only create a situation which *encourages* incorporation of writers' roles; we cannot create situations which *enforce* this response. Learning is in this sense very much a process of the learner, not the teacher. Teachers can only create contexts where it is likely to occur.

The question then becomes, "How can I, as a teacher, create a classroom where students are likely to identify writers' roles and incorporate them into their developing identity structure?" In the rest of this chapter, I would like to sketch an answer to this question by addressing (1) what classroom situations interfere with the identification and incorporation of writers' roles, (2) what situations present writers' roles so that they are likely to be identified and incorporated, and (3) what writers' roles might be important to present. I believe the answer to this question proposes a role we might consider as our mission in teaching writing.

Classroom Interference

To help students develop writers' roles which are useful for their wider cultural life, we need to present such roles in a way which allows them to be recognized and explored. In the courses described in chapters 3 and 4, the most powerful interference to such recognition is the traditional school roles of teacher-as-examiner and student-as-examinee. In courses where the student role was unclear and overemphasized, students were less able than in other courses to incorporate (or even identify) writers' roles. Classrooms which were structured so that the dominant way of understanding self was as student (as task performer writing for some sort of evaluation) interfered with the identification and incorporation of writers' roles.

Throughout all of the studies, an ongoing tension between student roles and writers' roles exists. In the audience-based class, the problematic student roles clearly created an interference to students' adoption of writers' roles. In the Piagetian ADAPT class, it was partly a tension over the implications of student and writer roles that led Joy Ritchie to change her teaching. In the workshop classes, many students articulated differences between the student expectations in this class and in other classes, most recognizing that in some ways the student roles in the workshop class were "easier" and therefore their grades in the course (high or low) were their own responsibility. In other words, throughout these classes student roles existed alongside or in conflict with writers' roles. The presentation and management of student roles had a lot to do with how students identified and incorporated writers' roles.

Intuitively, this enduring tension makes a good deal of sense. While in college, students are, after all, placed in the role of student by their presence in the institution. Their performance in classes turns into grades, which in time turn into a diploma. In an age when college diplomas are important for getting entry-level jobs in many professions, this institutional assignment of student roles is quite powerful. In contrast, the sorts of writers' roles presented in these classrooms (reflective writer, community influencer, publishing creative writer, and so forth) are not roles that function immediately within the school institution. They are roles that normally carry value in contexts other than classrooms.

For students to use their classroom experience to move from understanding themselves as students to understanding themselves as writers requires a shift in perceived context, a shift in how they understand the classroom where they are acting. Responding to cues presented in the classroom, they need to change their perception of classroom interaction from expected student-role purposes to purposes more centrally concerned with writers' behavior. Goffman (*Frame Analysis*) calls such shifts in perceived purposes for interaction "keying," using a musical metaphor of shifting keys to describe a social phenomenon "by which a given activity, one already meaningful in terms of some primary framework, is transformed into something patterned on this activity but seen by the participants to be something quite else" (43–44). Students in a "primary framework" of school interaction need to "transform" their understanding of that framework into a different, writerly framework. Writing in school, initially perceived as an activity designed to demonstrate that one is a successful or an unsuccessful student, needs to shift into an activity bearing implications for how one reflects on experience or communicates with and influences others. To make such a shift requires reconceptualizing one's classroom in a new way.

Such a reconceptualization does not happen by itself, of course. To make such a shift, people require some sort of mark or cue, some sort of indication that the other participants in the situation are also changing their understanding of the activity. Goffman calls such clues "keys" and points out that "keys" in social interaction are what tell us when someone is suggesting a shift in the understanding of context; for example, repeating someone else's words in falsetto is a "key" that one wants to shift the context from direct conversation to some sort of mockery of conversation.

Students need some cues in order to recognize shifts in how we understand classroom interaction. Without such cues, the normal expectations for classrooms remain in effect; and unless such cues come directly from the teacher, students will operate on the assumption that normal teacher-student roles are what the teacher expects. Since the normal teacher-student roles in our culture involve some sort of examiner-examinee relationship, students will expect that they will be graded on performance which demonstrates that they now know what the teacher already knows.

This student-to-teacher relationship of examinee-to-examiner has been well documented in many surveys of classrooms. In surveying high school writing classrooms, for example, Arthur Applebee and his team of researchers (*Contexts for Learning to Write*) found that most writing occurs as a form of examination, its purpose being to test a student's knowledge or performance on criteria the teacher establishes. Similarly, James Britton's study of writing development between ages 11 and 18 (*The Development of Writing Abilities 11–18*) showed that students most often write to an audience of teacher-as-examiner, and Frank Smith's study of K–12 literacy education (*Insult to Intelligence*) bemoans a prevalence of workbook and fill-in-the-blank instruction in language arts. Consequently, in the absence of explicit cues to the contrary, students will assume (on the basis of past experience) that their current teachers expect these same student roles.

The expected school roles for students lead students away from the possibility of writers' roles which involve contexts other than school. Unless student roles in the classroom are explicitly changed or "keyed," they will interfere with the identification and incorporation of writers' roles. Students need to experience a shift in how teacher and students interact, a change in the nature of student roles, if they are not to become fixed in the roles their past schooling leads them to expect.

It is important to make this point explicit because it is extremely difficult to recognize in practice. When I taught the audience-based class presented in chapter 3, for example, I believed I was doing the best I could to help students develop as writers because I had structured a sequence of exercises around an exciting and cutting-edge part of composition theory. I had worked hard to understand the concepts of audience and context, to form exercises which would make those concepts clear, and to present them to students in an engaging way. It was not until John Hendricks and I began trying to understand student response to the class that I could see how learning was trapped in the student roles my class had created. Instead of being able to learn concepts of audience in a way which applied directly to their concerns, students struggled to understand what kind of teacher-student roles were in operation in the class. They struggled to understand their roles as students instead of exploring writers' roles.

The power of social institutions to assign roles for people is very great, and school institutions assign roles for both teacher and student in powerful ways. As a young teacher, I had not imagined other structures for the classroom besides the "teacher makes assignments, students do them" structure I had experienced myself. Conscious labeling of roles and role expectations is not something we do readily, and that is why I needed something like John Hendricks's participant-observation in my course to perceive the roles I was presenting. In some ways the student-teacher roles in my classroom were more powerful than any of the material I taught, showing an aspect of what Giroux and Purpel call "the hidden curriculum" in operation.

According to Giroux and Purpel, schools provide an explicit curriculum of concepts and skills which students are to learn (often spelled out in documents like lesson plans, behavioral objectives, or the syllabus for a course like mine). But schools also provide a hidden curriculum of expectations for students' success and failure (never spelled out, but instead present in the way classroom interaction is structured, the way discipline is handled, and the way information is presented). The purpose of this hidden curriculum is to segment the populace into social classes by creating school interaction in such a way that students will, by an apparent self-selecting process of school success and failure, enter the culture's workforce in approximately the right numbers to maintain our classed society. Drawing on work like Paul Willis's *Learning to Labour: How Working Class Kids Get Working Class Jobs* and Shirley Brice Heath's *Ways with Words* (studies which detail how children from lower class backgrounds tend to disengage from school early on and then drop out during high school), Giroux and Purpel argue that the hidden curriculum for schools is set up not really to teach at all, but to segment the populace into an appropriate workforce.

From this perspective, the most frightening aspect of schooling is the fact that most teachers in our schools (certainly the teachers in the Willis and Heath studies) are well-meaning people who have devoted their lives to teaching as means of improving the next generation. The central problem of the hidden curriculum is how well-meaning teachers can unknowingly come to present students with unfreeing experiences while believing that they are offering students real help. How can people who care for students and want to help them end up serving as a tool for class segmentation? This problem, in many ways, was the problem I faced as a beginning teacher. I wanted to help my students learn to write, but the course I created served instead to continue a process that had started long ago for them—a process of deciding how long they were willing to play the student role, guessing the concepts the teacher would test for, in order to enter the workforce at a higher level.

Student roles, as traditionally understood, thus directly interfere with the identification and incorporation of writers' roles. As teachers, we can improve our teaching by clarifying for ourselves the kinds of roles we hope students will take on in our classrooms and the kinds of purposes for their learning which these roles include. Without providing explicit cues which show a shift in the nature of classroom roles, most of what we do will be perceived by students within the context of traditional examinee-to-examiner roles. The studies in this book (especially chapter 4) can provide teachers with examples of how teachers can perceive classroom roles and use their perceptions to change these roles.

Promoting Writers' Roles

In the studies in this book, writing workshops provided the clearest cues for shifting the perceived contexts of classroom interaction from student roles to writers' roles. As chapters 5 and 6 demonstrate, many students in these workshops came to identify and incorporate writers' roles into their self-understanding, and most students clearly recognized a shift from the traditional examinee-examiner version of student-teacher relationships. As a consequence, students were able to explore the writers' roles available in these classrooms and were able to find ways of incorporating aspects of these roles into their self-understanding. For some students, this exploration resulted in a recognition that they could use writing in ways they had not been able to before, identifying for themselves that a certain writer's role existed which they could take on if and when they found it important. For other students, this exploration resulted in a change in how they understood themselves, adding a new writer's role to the roles they intended to play in the future.

The reason these writing workshops were able to promote such changes was not that they had better concepts or material to teach than the other classes, or that the teachers were any better. Instead, the workshops created an environment where students' identity negotiations could focus on roles other than student roles because other roles were explicit, modeled, and visible. Student roles did exist, but they were simple, contractual roles which did not interfere with the exploration of writers' roles.

The workshop's expectations for students were, as many students pointed out, clear and easy. Instead of having to demonstrate that they knew what the teacher knows through tests, essay exams, or a sequence of work to master thinking skills, students merely had to do a certain amount of writing per week, take part in class and small group discussion, and finish a number of the pieces they had started during the course of the semester. Once they caught on to this contract for assigning grades, students recognized that it was a simple contract, one which they controlled and were responsible for. The contract which established the student-teacher relationship for grading was thus one cue that a different set of expectations for classroom interaction was in effect.

Because these student roles were clear, contractual, and easily dealt with, students were able to focus on other aspects of the class. Such things as the teacher taking part in activities along with students, bringing her own developing writing to share with the class, and working in small groups to read and respond to writing were cues which marked a shift in context from traditional classroom roles to a focus on writerly behavior. Similarly, the facts that students worked in small groups often without teacher intervention, that they chose their own topics and genres for writing, and that each week followed a predictable sequence of activities were cues that shifted the school context from a teacher-student examination context to a cooperative, community context. In the workshops, the opinions, ideas, and roles other students brought to the class functioned as a normal part of interaction, making much broader the range of perceived contexts in which course material operated.

While still occurring in a college classroom setting, the writing workshops allowed students to shift their focus, engagement, and motivation from restrictive student roles to other roles and interactions. They were able to observe their teacher's writerly behavior, the various ways their colleagues acted as writers, and their own writing in relation to contexts broader than the classroom. The setting allowed students to negotiate their understanding of writers' roles in a microcosm of many different versions of these roles, some presented by the teacher and some not.

The workshop setting, in short, allowed students to explore their writing in a way which connects with normal language learning, as researchers like Frank Smith describe it. Drawing on work in first language learning, Smith (*Insult to Intelligence*) points out that children normally learn language incidentally, as "a by product of the child's attempt to achieve some other end" such as joining the surrounding community, interacting with admired people, or getting some desired thing. Smith sets out three principles of learning writing which occur normally in language acquisition, principles which apply equally well to college students' learning in writing workshops:

1. Children not only learn the kinds of things that they see can be done with written language, as both reader and writer, but also explore how these particular things might be done. They are developing a world of literacy all the time. (34)
2. Children learn how written language is used from the way people in the community to which they belong use written language. (36)
3. Before learning to write children must first solve the problem of finding out what written language is for, what it does. Without this insight, no reading or writing instruction will ever make sense. Children solve this problem by making sense of the way people around them use written language. (36–37)

Like Smith's young children, college students in writing workshops are developing a world of literacy by exploring the ways people around them use written language, particularly by developing ideas about the purposes for writing from observing others. Instead of being "tested" on concepts or forms or processes through more or less elaborate examinations, students are able to explore the uses that writers make of writing, the behaviors of writers, and a range of purposes for their writing. Through this exploration, they are able to negotiate ways to identify or incorporate a writer's role into their self-understanding.

The studies in this book allow us to expand our understanding of why writing workshops can teach writing more effectively than other forms of teaching can. To the existing list of principles for workshop teaching, we can now add several additional principles which focus on roles and identity negotiations in workshops. In chapter 5, I listed four principles of workshops:

1. Ownership of writing
2. Predictable time spent on predictable activities
3. Response to writing in many modes
4. Presenting writing as a process

Structural in nature, these principles are aimed at guiding teachers in their attempts to organize writing workshops in their classrooms. To these principles, we can now add three others:

5. *Clear cues* which allow students to shift out of strict student-as-examinee, teacher-as-examiner roles, thereby eliminating the interference of the student role with writerly development
6. *Clear presentation of a variety of writers' roles* through demonstration, modeling, discussion, and interaction (the teacher as a writer is central in this principle, but equally important are the

opportunities to interact with roles other individuals bring to the classroom)

7. *Opportunities to try out and change roles*, to explore various ways the available writers' roles might be relevant to out-of-class experience

Writing workshops can allow teachers to present writers' roles to students in ways which allow identification and incorporation of those roles. By creating a context in which they are clearly presented (and not interfered with by student roles), workshop classes present students with real opportunities to learn writing—and to experience their learning in a way that can connect directly to their developing sense of self.

Important Writers' Roles

The courses I have described show clearly how certain student roles can interfere with learning to write and how writing workshops can successfully promote identification and incorporation of writers' roles. The courses also present a wide range of writers' roles for students to explore. In chapter 5 alone, for example, writers' roles as reflective thinker, community influencer, inspired genius, publishing creative writer, journalist, and report writer all appeared in the classroom with different degrees of emphasis. Some of these were presented directly by teacher behavior; others were presented by individual students with their own perspectives on writing.

A central question for writing teaching, consequently, is the question of what roles are best to present in writing classrooms so that students may have the opportunity to identify and incorporate them. What sort of writers' roles do students need to explore?

Obviously this question is a different kind of question than those addressed in the preceding sections of this chapter. In those sections, I could use direct evidence from student experience in studied classes to show that certain student roles interfere with learning and that writing workshops promote the identification and incorporation of writers' roles. But I do not have the same conclusive evidence in these studies for what writers' roles might be best for individual students, for groups of students taken together, or for our culture as a whole. My answer to this final question of what roles are best to present is therefore more speculative. I can only point out that the roles identified and explored by several students in the workshops bear some resemblance to writers' roles which many practicing writers describe for themselves—a convergence which suggests that the students in these classrooms may be on the right track.

In the workshop courses I have described, certain aspects of writers' roles appeared with some frequency in teacher presentation and student response. Joy and I presented writers' roles which focused on writing as a reflective activity for making sense of experience, writing as a communicative activity for influencing those in one's community, and writing as an aid for tolerance, for learning about and understanding opinions, values, and experiences different from one's own. Parts of these roles were identified and incorporated by different students.

In reading the work of practicing writers in our culture, I have been struck by how often these three aspects of writers' roles also appear. Many practicing writers describe their own writing experience as aimed at reflection, influencing their community, and promoting tolerance. For practicing writers, reflection on their place in society often leads to an identification of a need for some kind of understanding or tolerance, an identification which they then present in an attempt to influence their community. Let me illustrate this theme with a few examples.

When describing the genesis of their work, practicing writers often recount an initial point of reflection when they became aware of conflicts among the roles they play. Out of this conflict, they develop the ideas which lead to an attempt to influence society. Wendell Berry, a writer of essays about culture and agriculture, is an example of such a writer.

Berry lives on a farm in Port Royal and teaches at the University of Kentucky. Most of his writings concern agriculture and argue for traditional conceptions of family farms, Christian households, and land use. His writing is aimed at farmers and educators, especially those teaching at land-grant universities with colleges of agriculture. As a farmer and faculty member at such a university, he is a member of the groups he writes to, but his stance towards this membership shows a reflectiveness about the conflicts between his roles as farmer and professor:

> The commission said that the country's biggest problem was a surplus of farmers. . . . [They] had obviously taken for granted that the lives and communities of small farmers then still on the farm—and those of the 25 million who had left the farm since 1940—were of less value than "technological advances in agriculture." . . . Reading that article, I realized that my values were not only out of fashion, but under powerful attack. I saw that I was a member of a threatened minority. That is what set me off. (*The Unsettling of America* vi)

Berry's direct impetus for writing came from reflection, from his perception that agribusiness and agriculture professors were presenting ideas which harmed the lives of small farmers. Because he himself worked within both roles (agriculture professor and small farmer), the perception led to a desire to change the way his community understood agricultural issues. His sense of himself as "threatened minority," he says, is what set him off. Reflection, in other words, leads to writing as a means of influencing one's community.

I see a similar pattern of reflection leading to influence in the work of poet Audre Lorde. In a talk about the importance of developing one's own language for describing experience, Lorde claims the reflective and expressive power of language as a means of survival in a culture that needs change:

> I have come to believe over and over again that what is most important to me must be spoken, made verbal and shared, even at the risk of having it bruised and misunderstood. That the speaking profits me, beyond any other effect. I am standing here as a black lesbian poet. . . . And, of course, I am afraid—you can hear it in my voice—because the transformation of silence into language and action is an act of self-revelation and that always seems fraught with danger. . . . [As black women] we have had to fight and still do, for that very visibility which also renders us vulnerable, our blackness. For to survive in the mouth of this dragon we call america, we have had to learn this first and most vital lesson—that we were never meant to survive. (*The Cancer Journals* 19–21)

Lorde describes her work as a necessary consequence of reflecting on "who she is" in her culture. As a black lesbian poet, she is profoundly aware of her differences from mainstream Americans. These differences provide her with "what is most important" to be said, because in the recognition of these differences lies the possibility of change in the culture. This possibility of change is important because Lorde's differences are not simply unique. They are shared differences: her writing addresses and is supported by the groups of women who surround her, women "black and white, old and young, lesbian, bisexual, and heterosexual" who "all shared a war against the tyrannies of silence" (20). In other words, Lorde's work begins from a reflection on her roles in the culture and leads to a call for change, a call made possible by the support of a tolerant community of women like and unlike her.

Writers like Berry and Lorde seem to exhibit much the same understanding of writers' roles that developed in the workshops described in chapters 5 and 6. As writers, they begin with reflection, trying to understand their experience (particularly their experience in different roles in our culture); as their reflection leads to understanding, they write to influence their community, an influence often rooted in tolerance.

But there is another side to the experience of these writers. Along with the sense of reflection, attempted influence, and tolerance, they often describe a person who prompted them to write, someone who modeled for them writerly behavior and made it safe or possible. Lorde, for example, writes of the support she gained from a community of other women who were also speaking out against the tyrannies of silence. A behavioral model to follow, another human you respect who shows how to use language in ways you desire, is thus an equally important part of becoming a writer.

The most striking example I have found of the importance of such modeling is in Mary Daly's autobiographical preface to *The Church and the Second Sex*. Daly, a Roman Catholic theologian who developed a critique of the sexist practices of her church before finally leaving that church altogether, described her tension trying to reconcile her interest in theology and her mistreatment as a woman. In her preface, she says she only considered writing a woman's critique of the church because the experience of the Second Vatican Council made her feel that such a critique might be heard and because another female theologian modeled that behavior for her:

> It was not only the experience of the Vatican council in Rome that made this written expression of anger and hope possible. Another important catalyst had been an article by Rosemary Lauer, a Catholic philosopher, which appeared two years earlier in *Commonweal*. That piece had been only moderately critical of the church's treatment of women, but the fact that a woman who retained her identity as "Catholic" had said these things was an astounding breakthrough. It somehow bestowed upon me the psychological freedom to "write out loud" my own thoughts. (10)

As Daly describes it, her experience in writing her book came directly out of reflection on the conflicts between her roles as woman and Catholic (an experience similar to Berry's and Lorde's). But her writing only became possible when she saw, by reading Lauer's article, that a woman could be both Catholic and critical. Her writing only became possible when the role was modeled for her. Her ability to influence her community through writing emerged because of this reflection and modeling.

Adrienne Rich, one of the many writers who taught with Mina Shaughnessy in the initial State University of New York basic writing program, likewise focused on the importance of such modeling behavior in claiming writers' roles for the self. In many of her articles in *On Lies, Secrets, and Silence,* Rich describes writers who have modeled behavior for her, thereby influencing her own development: Anne Sexton, Judy Grahn, Emily Dickinson. As a teacher in the basic writing program, she said she was most excited by the possibility of offering to her students the same power in language these writers offered her. In describing this possibility of language, Rich points directly to the reflective, community-influencing, modeling power of becoming a writer:

> What has held me, and what I think holds many who teach basic writing . . . is the possibility that many of these young men and women may be gaining the kind of *critical perspective on their lives* [reflection] and the *skill to bear witness* [modeling; community influencing] that they have never before had in our country's history. At the bedrock of my thinking about this is the sense that language is power, and that, as Simone Weil says, those who suffer from injustice most are the least able to articulate their suffering; and that the silent majority, if released into language, would not be content with a perpetuation of the conditions which have betrayed them. This notion hangs on a special conception of what it means to be released into language: not simply learning the jargon of an elite, fitting unexceptionally into the status quo, but *learning that language can be a means of changing reality* [community influencing]. What interests me is less the emergence of the occasional genius than the overall finding of language by those who did not have it and by those who have been used and abused to the extent that they lacked it. (67–68; my emphasis)

This passage points directly to the act of writing as an act of reflecting, influencing, and claiming a social place—even of changing the social fabric of a culture so that new positions might arise. Like Lorde, Rich presents her own position as both contrary to and connected to the surrounding culture: contrary to "the elite" but connected to other "basic writing teachers" who work, as she does, for the possibility of a new social order. Rich in fact links her students' claiming of writing to the creation of this new order: language, she says, is a means of changing reality, and through writing her students can develop a critical perspective on their lives and the potential to bear witness for the groups they represent. In other words, Rich is aware that her students, if they proceed as writers, can model for others an empowering stance towards experience and aware that her own classroom is a place where such modeling occurs. She is aware that students in her classes have to negotiate a stance towards writing and consequently that her class can help or hinder them. Some students (she hopes) will come to claim writing as a means of critical reflection and change, others (she fears) will only view writing as a means of entering a higher social class, and still others (she knows) will reject writing because of the failures and unacceptable values it presents to them. In each case, the power of writing as reflection and influence is at stake.

This brief survey of what practicing writers say about writing shows great similarity to what college students were beginning to say in the writing workshops. Writers like Berry, Lorde, Daly, and Rich describe their writers' roles in terms of reflection on the roles they play and attempts to influence their culture. Similarly, students like Tim (chapter 5) and Becky (chapter 6) describe themselves developing roles for the self as reflective writer; students like Brad (chapter 6) and Bob (chapter 5) describe themselves developing roles as community influencer. Practicing writers also describe a need for a supportive, tolerant community and for models of the sorts of people they are trying to become. Similarly, students like Tim describe the power of their classes as supportive but pluralistic communities, and students like Brad point to the important ways their teachers modeled writerly behavior for them.

While I cannot say at all securely from these studies what sort of writers' roles we ought to present to students, I can say that such convergences between how practicing writers and students in writing workshops describe themselves lead me to believe that such students are on the right track. Given that the practicing writers I have described all see improving their culture as at least part of their purpose for writing, these convergences between students' and writers' descriptions lead me to believe that workshop classes may also be promoting a kind of active engagement in the culture which can only prove beneficial.

In sum, the identity negotiation perspective I have presented in this book can help us understand our teaching mission more thoroughly. Teaching writing in writing classrooms is not an isolated activity in our lives, our students' lives, or the life of our culture. Instead, the roles we experience and explore in classrooms are connected to the development of our selves and our culture. The people we become individually and collectively are influenced by our classroom interaction. As the studies in this book show, our classrooms can help promote the identification and incorporation of writers' roles, or they can continue to limit such role development by fixing school interaction within narrow student-teacher roles. Our students will always negotiate understandings of the value and importance of what we teach in relation to the roles operating in our classrooms. It is up to us, as teachers of writing, to let some of those roles encourage the development of writerly behavior and civic participation.

If these studies accomplish nothing else, they should at least show teachers that the roles which operate in their classrooms will indeed influence the way students learn. By observing the roles available in our own classrooms, we can describe how our students are learning and the kinds of selves we are helping them to become. Such observation, finally, offers us teachers a choice: what roles will we promote? what sorts of selves will we help our students to develop? The choice is, of course, ours, and aspects of our culture's future depend on the choices we will make. An identity negotiations perspective can make these choices clear; the rest is up to us, our students, and the kinds of writing classes we create.

References

ADAPT Program. *Multidisciplinary Piagetian-Based Programs for College Freshmen.* Lincoln: ADAPT, 1977.

Annas, Pamela. "Style as Politics: A Feminist Approach to the Teaching of Writing." *College English* 49 (1987): 360–79.

Applebee, Arthur, with contributions by Judith Langer, et al. *Contexts for Learning to Write: Studies for Secondary School Instruction.* Norwood, N.J.: Ablex, 1984.

Aronowitz, Stanley, and Henry Giroux. *Education under Siege: The Conservative, Liberal, and Radical Debate over Schooling.* Granby, Mass.: Bergin and Garvey, 1985.

Atwell, Nancie. *In the Middle: Writing, Reading, and Learning with Adolescents.* Upper Montclair, N.J.: Boynton/Cook, 1987.

Bazerman, Charles. "What Written Knowledge Does: Three Examples of Academic Discourse." *Philosophy of the Social Sciences* 11 (1981): 361–87.

Belenky, Mary Field, Blythe McVicker Clinchy, Nancy Rule Goldberger, and Jill Mattuck Tarule. *Women's Ways of Knowing: The Development of Self, Voice, and Mind.* New York: Basic Books, 1986.

Berlin, James. "Contemporary Composition: The Major Pedagogical Theories." *College English* 44 (1982): 756–77.

Berry, Wendell. *The Unsettling of America: Culture and Agriculture.* San Francisco: Sierra Club Books, 1977.

Berthoff, Ann E. *The Making of Meaning.* Upper Montclair, N.J.: Boynton/Cook, 1981.

Bizzell, Patricia. "Arguing about Literacy." *College English* 50 (1988): 141–53.

————. "Cognition, Convention, and Certainty: What We Need to Know about Writing." *Pre/Text* 3 (1982): 213–43.

Britton, James, Tony Burgess, Nancy Martin, Alex McLeod, and Harold Rosen. *The Development of Writing Abilities (11–18).* London: Macmillan, 1975.

Brooke, Robert. "Modeling a Writer's Identity: Reading and Imitation in the Writing Classroom." *College Composition and Communication* 39 (1988): 23–41.

————. "Underlife and Writing Instruction." *College Composition and Communication* 38 (1987): 141–53.

157

————. "Writing and Commitment: Some Psychosocial Functions of College Writing." Ph.D. diss. University of Minnesota, 1984.

Brooke, Robert, and John Hendricks. *Audience Expectations and Teacher Demands*. Carbondale, Ill.: Conference on College Composition and Communication/Southern Illinois University Press, 1989.

Brooke, Robert, Tom O'Connor, and Ruth Mirtz. "Leadership in College Writing Groups." *Writing on the Edge* 1 (1989): 66–86.

Calkins, Lucy McCormick. *The Art of Teaching Writing*. Portsmouth, N.H.: Heinemann, 1986.

————. *Lessons from a Child on the Teaching and Learning of Writing*. Portsmouth, N.H.: Heinemann, 1983.

Coles, William E., Jr. *The Plural I: The Teaching of Writing*. New York: Holt, Rinehart, and Winston, 1978.

Connors, Robert J. "Personal Writing Assignments." *College Composition and Communication* 38 (1987): 166–83.

Craig, R., and K. Tracy, eds. *Conversational Coherence: Form, Structure, and Strategy*. Beverly Hills, Calif.: Sage, 1983.

Daly, Mary. *The Church and the Second Sex*. Boston: Beacon Press, 1985.

de Beaugrande, Robert. *Text, Discourse, and Process: Towards a Multidisciplinary Science of Texts*. Norwood, N.J.: Ablex, 1980.

Elbow, Peter. *Embracing Contraries: Explorations in Learning and Teaching*. New York: Oxford University Press, 1986.

————. *Writing with Power: Techniques for Mastering the Writing Process*. New York: Oxford University Press, 1981.

————. *Writing without Teachers*. New York: Oxford University Press, 1973.

Erikson, Erik. *Childhood and Society*. New York: Norton, 1950.

————. *Identity: Youth and Crisis*. New York: Norton, 1968.

Fetterley, Judith. *The Resisting Reader: A Feminist Approach to American Fiction*. Bloomington: Indiana University Press, 1978.

Flower, Linda. *Problem Solving Strategies for Writing*. New York: Harcourt Brace Jovanovich, 1982.

Foucault, Michel. *Discipline and Punish: The Birth of the Prison*. New York: Random House, 1977.

Freire, Paulo. *Education for Critical Consciousness*. New York: Seabury, 1973.

————. *Pedagogy for the Oppressed*. New York: Continuum, 1970.

Geertz, Clifford. *The Interpretation of Cultures*. New York: Basic Books, 1973.

————. *Local Knowledge: Further Essays in Interpretive Anthropology*. New York: Basic Books, 1983.

————. *Works and Lives: The Anthropologist as Author*. Stanford: Stanford University Press, 1988.

Giroux, Henry A. *Teachers as Intellectuals: Toward a Critical Pedagogy of Learning*. Granby, Mass.: Bergin and Garvey, 1988.

————. *Theory and Resistance in Education*. Granby, Mass.: Bergin and Garvey, 1988.

Giroux, Henry, and David Purpel. *The Hidden Curriculum and Moral Education*. Berkeley: McCutchan, 1983.

Goffman, Erving. *Asylums: Essays on the Social Situation of Mental Patients and Other Inmates*. Chicago: Aldine Publishing Company, 1961.

––––––. *Frame Analysis: An Essay on the Organization of Experience*. New York: Harper and Row, 1974.

––––––. *Interaction Ritual: Essays on Face to Face Behavior*. New York: Pantheon, 1967.

––––––. *Relations in Public: Microstudies of the Public Order*. New York: Harper and Row, 1971.

––––––. *Stigma: Notes on the Management of Spoiled Identity*. Englewood Cliffs, N.J.: Prentice-Hall, 1963.

Graves, Donald. *A Researcher Learns to Write*. Portsmouth, N.H.: Heinemann, 1984.

Heath, Shirley Brice. *Ways with Words: Language, Life, and Work in Communities and Classrooms*. New York: Cambridge University Press, 1983.

Holland, Norman. *The I*. New Haven: Yale University Press, 1985.

Kantor, Kenneth J. "Classroom Contexts and the Development of Writing Intentions: An Ethnographic Case Study." In *New Directions in Composition Research*, edited by Richard Beach and Lillian Bridwell, 72–94. New York: Guilford Press, 1984.

Kantor, Kenneth J., Dan R. Kirby, and Judith P. Goetz. "Research in Context: Ethnographic Studies in English Education." *Research in the Teaching of English* 15 (1981): 293–309.

Kennedy, X., and D. Kennedy. *The Bedford Reader*. 2nd ed., New York: St. Martin's, 1985.

Labov, William. *Language in the Inner City*. Philadelphia: Pennsylvania University Press, 1972.

Laing, R. D. *The Divided Self*. New York: Pantheon, 1960.

––––––. *The Politics of Experience*. New York: Pantheon, 1967.

––––––. *Self and Others*. New York: Pantheon, 1961.

––––––. *The Voice of Experience*. New York: Pantheon, 1982.

Laing, R. D., and A. Esterson. *Sanity, Madness, and the Family: Families of Schizophrenics*. 2nd ed. New York: Basic Books, 1971.

Lauer, Janice M. and Michael Carter. *Four Worlds of Writing*. New York: Harper and Row, 1981.

Laurence, Margaret. *A Bird in the House*. Toronto: Seal, 1978.

Lorde, Audre. *The Cancer Journals*. San Francisco: Spinsters Ink, 1980.

Marcus, George E., and Michael M. J. Fischer. *Anthropology as Cultural Critique: An Experimental Moment in the Human Sciences*. Chicago: University of Chicago Press, 1986.

Mitchell, Ruth, and Mary Taylor. "The Integrating Perspective: An Audience-Response Model for Writing." *College English* 41 (1979): 247–71.

Moffett, James. *Active Voice: A Writing Program Across the Curriculum*. Upper Montclair, N.J.: Boynton/Cook, 1981.

Murray, Donald. *A Writer Teaches Writing.* 2nd ed. Boston: Houghton Mifflin, 1985.

North, Stephen. *The Making of Knowledge in Composition: Portrait of an Emerging Field.* Upper Montclair, N.J.: Boynton/Cook, 1987.

Rich, Adrienne. *On Lies, Secrets, and Silence: Selected Prose 1966–1978.* New York: Norton, 1979.

Rose, Mike. "The Language of Exclusion: Writing Instruction at the University." *College English* 47 (1987): 341–59.

—————. *Lives on the Boundary: The Struggles and Achievements of America's Underprepared.* New York: Free Press, 1988.

Slugoski, B. R., and G. P. Ginsburg. "Ego Identity and Explanatory Speech." In *Texts of Identity*, edited by John Shotter and Kenneth Gergen, 36–55. Newbury Park, Calif.: Sage, 1989.

Smith, Frank. *Insult to Intelligence: The Bureaucratic Invasion of Our Classrooms.* Portsmouth, N.H.: Heinemann, 1986.

Willis, Paul. *Learning to Labour: How Working Class Kids Get Working Class Jobs.* Lexington, Mass.: D.C. Heath, 1977.

Vygotsky, Lev. *Thought and Language.* Cambridge, Mass.: M.I.T. Press, 1962.

Young, Richard, Alton Becker, and Kenneth Pike. *Rhetoric: Discovery and Change.* Harcourt Brace Jovanovich, 1970.

Author

Robert Brooke grew up in Denver, Colorado, and attended Gonzaga University and the University of Minnesota. He is an associate professor at the University of Nebraska–Lincoln, where he works with the composition program and the Nebraska Writing Project. His publications include *Audience Expectations and Teacher Demands* and essays in *College Composition and Communication* and *College English.* In 1988 he received the Richard Braddock Award for his article "Underlife and Writing Instruction." He is currently working on theories and pedagogies of response to writing.

Joy Ritchie is an assistant professor at the University of Nebraska–Lincoln and codirector of the Nebraska Writing Project. She teaches undergraduate and graduate courses in composition and is currently writing about the connections between composition and feminist theory. She has published articles in *College Composition and Communication* and *The Journal of Advanced Composition.*

Index

163